Richard —
always go for the
total return.

Regards,

2/91

PLUGGING INTO UTILITIES

A Safe and Sound Way to Superior Returns

IN THE
STOCK MARKET

DONALD L. CASSIDY

PROBUS PUBLISHING COMPANY
Chicago, Illinois
Cambridge, England

ISBN 1-55738-498-3

Printed in the United States of America

BB

1   2   3   4   5   6   7   8   9   0

To Belita, my bride,
who has loved me enough to give me
the space and time to keep writing

Table of

Part III IMPLEMENTING THE MASTER PLAN

Part IV ISSUES AND TACTICS

AUTHOR'S NOTE

Acknowledgements

A second book, be assured, is an immensely easier and less frightening undertaking than a first. The writer knows it can be done, because it has been done previously. This knowledge provides the push and the energy to keep the work moving forward. But the author's efforts alone are not sufficient. There are many who deserve thanks.

Belita Calvert, my loving wife and new bride, in her heart would rather have me all to herself rather than share me with the library, a database, and a personal computer. But she understands that I get great pleasure from work and from writing and from the opportunity to teach, so she has generously given me the space and time needed.

Several colleagues and good friends from the Denver office of Lipper Analytical Services, Inc., have my thanks as well. They are, alphabetically, Geoffrey Bobroff, Evelyn Carter, Patrick DeMera, and Korey Weiser. Without their patience and flexibility regarding my sometimes-trying writing schedule juggled against constant work/publishing deadlines, I would not have been able to finish on time — or perhaps ever. They have been most kind and tolerant of my "outside job."

J. Michael Jeffers, president of the publisher, deserves special recognition for having launched my book-writing career in 1989 by acquiring the manuscript of my first volume, *It's Not What Stocks You Buy, It's When You Sell That Counts: Understanding and Overcoming Your Self-Imposed Barriers to Investment Success.* I thank him for his courage and foresight in backing a treatment of an offbeat topic where others might have demurred.

A number of former colleagues at Boettcher & Company, now a division of Kemper Securities, Inc., were helpful in ways neither they nor I understood at the time. Richard Follingstad of Albuquerque, and Flem Currin and Joe Ballantyne of Tucson were kind enough to let me expose controversial opinions (advice to sell the local utility's stocks) to their offices' clients. And Debra Silversmith, as Research Director, did not inhibit my writing adverse reports — more than could be said for some in her place at other firms.

Finally, through seminars based on my earlier book, I have had the pleasure of meeting and exchanging thoughts with dozens of stockbrokers and hundreds of individual investors in a dozen states, who have provided useful insight—sometimes quite unintentionally. The formation of investment thought is, after all, a two-way street.

PART ONE

OVERVIEW: YOU AND UTILITY INVESTING

The Objective: Profit and Security, Not Thrills

People buy stocks for a number of reasons. Judged in the cold light of rationality, many of those reasons are ill-advised and downright self-destructive. Purely from the perspective of an investment objective, there are just two reasons why a person should buy common stocks. True equities investing, as most textbooks on the subject proclaim, is oriented toward prospective cash income. The process consists of identifying those companies whose stocks are undervalued in terms of future earning power. One buys them because the projected earnings stream will produce a stream of presumably rising dividends. This objective is the absolute core of the rationale for investing in utility shares.

The second reason is to seek growth in capital. Higher prices are likely over time if the fortunes of the underlying company improve, if interest rates decline, and if psychology in the stock market generally (or toward the industry group in particular) moves from negative toward positive. One buys stocks in order to sell them at a profit in the future. Investing in utilities can include this component, and if properly executed it will contribute appreciably to the total return achieved.

The two drivers of stock price are the dividend stream itself and the rate at which the market capitalizes that stream. Much of this book focuses on the process of selecting, buying, holding, and, when appropriate, selling utility stocks based on the first driver, their dividend trends. Thus, some of the capital appreciation anticipated to be part of the total return will be driven by dividend growth. The second source of potential capital gain is riding the interest rate cycle successfully. Much more can be

1

achieved this way than by gritting one's teeth and riding out the storm for several years at a time. In Section III Implementation, a chapter is devoted to riding the main cycles (Chapter 18).

While many investors *say* they are buying or holding a stock for potential capital growth, this easy generalization is too commonly a psychological cover for their true motivation. The following are some of the real underlying motivations of these "investors:"

LOYALTY. Some people buy shares of the company for which they work, or of a prominent employer enterprise in the community in which they live. A loyalty-based purchase is not timed to investment value but is generated merely by the buyer's awareness and liquidity. This approach can result in major investment losses since there is a tendency for loyalty to override common sense and therefore to prevent timely or prudent sale. Both the buying and selling decisions tend to be poorly timed and therefore badly priced.

AFFILIATION. Others will buy a stock because of a perceived closeness with the members of management or because they like the products or services the company offers. A recent example was a Utah-based grocery chain whose shares were first sold to the public in the summer of 1989. Many local residents bought the stock, which was sold in the initial public offering ("IPO") at $19 a share. Three weeks later it had risen to $24. That quick profit was abnormal and should have been nailed down by purely rational holders. But very few holders sold out. Why? The company was well respected and clearly successful, but more important, many senior members of management, like many of the Utah-based buyers, were Mormons. So the investors felt unable to break this strong link by selling the stock. These kinds of investment decisions are usually not timed or made on a price/value basis. They simply are not primarily driven by the profit motive, so it is mostly academic to discuss them in that context.

STORY OR CONCEPT. Many — too many — stock purchases are made because of excitement over a concept. In many cases either the purchaser is ignorant of investment values and just "feels good" owning a company that is involved in the subject business (environmental protection, humane research on new drugs, AIDS, etc.) or has purchased the stock to feel trendy or part of an "in crowd." People who make concept purchases say they expect to prosper from them. But enthusiasm overrides logic, and losses are much more common than gains. Typically, the danger to financial success is that the concept remains alive in the mind well after the likelihood of a price rise has passed.

THRILL OF THE GAME. There are also many, many people who buy stocks mostly for the thrill of participation in the game. They play the market because it is socially acceptable (and sometimes socially required or expected) to do so. These people play to play, but not necessarily with a consuming drive to win. The market is a way of getting the thrills and emotional rollercoaster ride of a gambler but more gradually, for a longer period of time, and legally. The Wall Street game feels "cleaner" than a trip to Las Vegas or Atlantic City or a call to the bookmaker.

PSYCHOLOGICAL LOSERS. There is almost undoubtedly a subcategory of buyers for emotional reasons consisting of masochists and neurotics. These people, for reasons the author is not fully qualified to explore, actually have a need to punish themselves and/or others and subconsciously "plan" to lose money with their investments. Their patterns of financial failure tend to repeat.

DIAGNOSIS

Investing in utility shares should be a process born purely of serious conservative investment motivation. There is no thrill to be had. Those who buy other investments for (at least in part) any of the nonfinancial reasons noted above will be bored and frustrated with utilities. They simply should not play in this corner of the market, and by and large they do not.

The reader should carefully examine his or her own history of investing to detect any of the patterns described above. If they exist, make a decision to separate the funds devoted to income investing for retirement from the "fun money" allocated to the nonfinancial psychological games of Wall Street. It is critical that the two pots of money be physically separated as between two brokerage firms, or between the personal account and the IRA, for example. It is also critical never to transfer money from the serious category to the play fund. Doing that robs the investor of part of the target standard of living in retirement and is the beginning of the end of all discipline. Ruin will follow, sooner or later.

The investor for retirement income using utilities must set an objective. Simply stated, that objective must be superior profit or rate of return with low risk over a sustained period. The plan for reaching the goal should be written down and referred to periodically, for reinforcement. One should read it at least quarterly and each time a transaction is about to be made. There can be no deviation, no lapses in self-discipline, no rationalizations of foolhardy side trips into investment story-or fantasyland. The plan must state a clear monetary objective and must enunciate realistic means of achieving it. For example, the plan might be to accumulate $200,000 by age 65 to provide a presumed $15,000 annual income starting at that time with no capital depletion. Therefore there must be annual contributions of so many dollars, and the fund must be programmed to grow at an attainable average rate of "X" percent per year. The annual contributions will be determined by the assumed investment rate, the time to age 65, and the size of any starting fund.

The primary component of a successful investment program is not taking big gains, but simply avoiding losses. The cost of losses is huge, especially when they occur early in the plan. By contrast, and fortunately, the power of compounding is very great, especially when allowed to operate for long periods. For these reasons it is critical to adhere to the plan strictly. This means making the annual contributions on schedule, not diverting funds into high-risk alternatives no matter how apparently attractive, and following prudent rules for liquidating positions before they become bigger problems and generate losses — or when yields become too low to justify the capital risk of further holding.

These topics are covered in some detail in subsequent chapters. In particular, there is a focus on the choice between high current yield (an ever-present temptation) versus the lower risk and greater certainty of accepting a lower cash yield in exchange for better total return. This book also develops a system for making the buy/hold/avoid/sell decision on utility common stocks based on their dividend trends. It will be most important that the investor adhere to rules, rejecting rationalization, when signals call for action.

There is a reason that you, the reader, bought or borrowed this volume. The reason is that, deep in your mind and heart, you know that get-rich-quick investment programs do not work and will bring ruin in the long run, just as a gambler's hot streak always ends. You know that slow and steady wins the race, not fast and flashy. You know that a disciplined program based on common sense and reality will work in the long run. And you realize that your future standard of living is (literally!) what's at stake in the game. How you live, what you can give the grandchildren, where and how often you can travel—all these will be based on your investment success, not on Social Security alone. So you are ready to break bad past habits, create and fund a program for your own longterm future, and "get down to business." What we are talking about is serious money, YOUR serious money!

In short, you the reader, have decided it is time to take action. The key to being on the right path is to keep the objective in sight: the goal is profit, not thrills. Put away your gambling instincts, and get ready for a sometimes humdrum but cumulatively rewarding investment experience. Whenever you are tempted to stray from the conservative path, recite the following: "I am playing with my retirement money here. I cannot afford to lose." That sobering focus should serve you well. Go for the gold, not for the glory!

Rule #1: Preserve Capital

WHY LOSING MONEY IS EVEN WORSE THAN YOU THOUGHT

The time value of money should be a central consideration for every investor. At its core, this concept means that a dollar today is worth more than a dollar a year from now, and not only because of the seemingly insatiable appetite of inflation. Even more basically, a dollar today can be turned into a dollar plus several cents in a year if left at interest. The primary objective of participating in the securities market, of course, is to make profits beyond what can be had through the operation of compound interest in the bank. Lend a bank your money and it will put part of those dollars into securities to take advantage of the interest spread. (When you participate in the market, ups and downs must be expected, but the hope is that the main trend will be up. Superior total return over time, meaning capital growing faster than it would in risk-free investments such as the bank or T-bills, is the goal.)

Here is an absolutely central concept never to forget: The key to making big money in equity investing, contrary to the titles of the dozen-plus new books that appear each year, is *not* in making the big gain. The key is: *not losing* money.

The overriding importance of not losing money, as opposed to making fast money, is highlighted by this true story. A young, bright, and eager investment analyst was granted an audience with a highly successful, near legendary Texas-based money manager. The elder controlled several billion dollars of other people's invested funds for a major bank. Befitting his accomplishments, his office was spacious, the furniture and carpeting rich. The view of the city skyline was spectacular. He could have had virtually any office art hanging on the walls that he cared to order. The young analyst seeking wisdom from the guru expected piles of charts and books and a blackboard scrawled with secret investment formulae. However, on display in the large office he found but one small item, modestly framed. Nothing else on all four walls. Just a little 6x9 inch plaque, reading:

There are 2 rules for successful investing:
Rule #1: Never lose money.
Rule #2: Always follow rule #1.

The more constant the attention an investor pays to not losing money, the more disciplined and therefore more successful he or she will be. The caution involved in buying and selling with loss prevention first in mind makes this approach work systematically and gradually over the long pull. There are no thrills nor overnight killings; any windfalls are strictly pleasant surprises. The cold truth of investment mathematics works relentlessly *for*, rather than against, the investor whose program is centered on avoiding loss.

In order to succeed at not losing money, an investor must deal with objective realities as much as possible and must identify and reject the emotional, the irrelevant, and the misleading. The utilities investment arena, fortunately, makes this process less difficult than with most other types of stocks. If a stock in most other industries is in an overall declining trend, rallies in price or good fundamental news items that do not reverse the trend serve only to create false hope. Such developments encourage the owner to hold on because "prosperity is just around the corner." Similarly, if the trend of interest rates (often driven by inflation) is up, the prices of utility investments will fall. Period. Even the most healthy companies' securities are then good sales, to be bought back later when the macro tide reverses to a favorable direction. With utilities, the signposts are simple: earnings drive the growth rate in dividends; directors' dividend actions confirm the story; interest rates put a market value on the dividend stream.

KINDS OF LOSSES

A successful investment is defined not merely by its result as reported for tax purposes. Other key measures are subsequent action of the stock sold and the actions of other available investments. If a sold stock goes down or sideways in price, or even if it goes up less than the general market (adjusted for beta, for purist readers!), then the sale was a well-executed decision, a success. So the concept that economists call opportunity cost is part of the measure of winning or losing. For example, even if inflation were zero, a person holding excess money in a checking account takes a loss by not transferring it to savings to gather interest.

There are really several dimensions to obeying rule #1. The first, in an idealized world, is to buy only stocks that do not go down. (Will Rogers is reputed to have said "Making money in the market is easy: just find stocks that go up and buy them." Even if it were that simple, he'd have missed entirely the concept of opportunity cost, which is always less obvious than the kind of loss that is recorded on Form 1040 Schedule D.

Another and more subtle kind of opportunity loss is related to the time value of money. The investor feels sick when a stock goes from 20 to 12. One feels unlucky when it goes from 20 to 30, only to back off to 22, but probably not quite as bad. But chances are that one feels little if any real pain when the stock sits at 20, and sits and sits. Or, more realistically, when the stock fluctuates around 20 for a prolonged period of time. A stock going nowhere, although not as damaging as a stock shrinking in price, is nevertheless a source of opportunity loss, since it is frittering away the one nonrenewable resource in life: time. While that investment meanders around the familiar $20 level, the time remaining before the investor's retirement age or college funding deadline is shortening. Without accepting an improperly high level of risk, one cannot make up for lost time. The compounded value of the early-lost money is effectively gone forever. Only decreased current consumption can replace the investment fund's shortage. And such an alternative reduces the current quality of life. The investor's choice: pay back the loss now, or pay for it later.

The stagnant-money loss is the most insidious because it is the least painful. How many times have you heard a friend, or your broker, or even yourself(!) say "Hey, at least I didn't *lose* money!"? If that's your attitude, you should be in CDs and not bother buying books on investing. A dead-money loss is measured in severity by the amount of time squandered. Not losing is not good enough.

In investing, time can be a very powerful ally; by the same token, the cost of lost time can become staggering. Compound interest works in wondrous ways, if the investor actually allows it to work. Table 2.1 shows the amount of $1,000 after various periods of years if compounded at the annual rates listed.

Table 2.1 Value of $1,000 with Varying Rates of Increase and Time Periods			
Rate of Increase Per Year			
@8%	@10%	@12%	@15%
10 Years $2,159	$2,594	$3,106	$4,046
20 Years $4,661	$6,727	$9,646	$16,366
30 years $10,063	$17,449	$29,960	$66,211
40 Years $21,724	$45,259	$93,050	$267,861

Such numbers are commonly produced by banks and mutual funds to encourage the public to invest. But for purposes of this chapter, think about the flip side: the amounts above are how much *less* will end up in your retirement fund for every $1,000 loss taken early in life. That's for every thousand not put into the fund or for every thousand lost through bad investments. Pretty sobering numbers.

Remember that capital sums such as those shown in the table represent, by implication at reasonable interest rates, certain retirement income streams. Thus, for example, if $1,000 is lost at age 45 and the fund would have earned 12% per annum, retirement income at age 65 is reduced by $1,157 per year forever, and the estate is cut by the $9,646 shown. Make that $1,000 investment error at age 25, and the cost in retirement *income* is $11,166 per year or almost $1,000 *per month* for life! *Plus* some $93,050 not passed on to the heirs. Remember, the goal of a retirement-oriented program is to build capital, not to take the chances that might produce thrills along the way. And the best way to build capital dependably for a serious objective, like living comfortably in retirement, is to avoid losses.

A dead-money loss, or worse yet a real-dollar loss, imposes another subtle but dangerous burden on the conservative investor. To recoup lost time and money, one is tempted to stray into high-risk territory. This can lead to disaster for the conservative investor. The mirage of high yield is all too often the yield-oriented investor's downfall (more on this in Chapter 11).

WHAT IS A REASONABLE RETURN? SOME HISTORY

Ask a dozen investors what a realistic return rate is and expect a dozen answers, all of them subjective and many probably wishful. Probably the most widely cited study of actual long-term stock-market performance is that by Roger Ibbotson and Rex Sinquefield *(Stocks, Bonds, Bills, and Inflation: the Past (1926-1976) and the Future (1977-2000)*; Charlottsville, VA., Financial Analysts Research Foundation, 1977), which examined returns on financial instruments over a half century. This monumental study's conclusion was that over a very long period of time common stocks provide higher average returns than the other investment media covered. The average rate for common stocks for 1926 through 1976 was not 25% or 20% or even 15%, but 9.2% per annum. This return included both capital appreciation and dividends. The 9.2% figure is useful for making a key point about the time value of money.

Most investors are familiar with the so-called "Rule of 72," a convenient mathematical oddity that easily tells how long it takes to double a sum of money at annual compounded rates. It is not totally precise, but it is operationally close enough within realistic ranges of time and return. As shown in Table 2.2, what the "Rule of 72" says is that 72 is (very nearly exactly) the mathematical product of the percentage interest rate and the number of years that it takes to double a sum of money left to compound. Actually there are three ways to look at the "Rule of 72":

• Years times rate equals (pretty nearly) 72, or

• 72 divided by rate equals number of years required; or

• 72 divided by available years equals rate required to double a sum.

Table 2.2 Time to Double Money: The Rule of 72			
Years	Rule-Implied Rate in %	Multiple of Starting Sum	Actual Rate to Double
3	24	1.907	26%
4	18	1.939	18.9
5	14.4	1.959	14.9
6	12	1.974	12.25
7	10.3	1.986	10.4
8	9	1.993	9.05
9	8	1.999	8
10	7.2	2.004	7.2
11	6.5	1.999	6.5
12	6	2.012	5.95
13	5.5	2.006	5.5
14	5.1	2.006	5.1

All investors have been told about cutting losses and letting profits run. The time value of money is one of the two reasons underlying that cliché (the other is culling the dogs). Suppose a conservative investor were to settle for the long-term equities return of 9.2% per annum. Table 2.2 shows what happens if the portfolio or single issue merely stands still. After one year of stagnation, the then-required average annual compounded return to get back on schedule and double in eight years becomes 10.4% over the remaining seven years (moving up the first column one line to shorter time periods to locate the required returns in the fourth column).

That is not too dramatic. However, after two years of zero progress, the required catchup return rate for the remaining six years jumps to 12.25%. And that is fully 35% more than the 9% required originally to double one's money, and some 33% better than the long-term mean rate discovered by Ibbotson and Sinquefield — a 33% overperformance that then must be accomplished *for the next six years running*. This is the stark implication of being patient with an investment going nowhere. When investments are not working out, patience is a fault rather than a virtue.

But the really big damage comes when a loss occurs. Table 2.3 shows what happens when a loss of capital is sustained, and especially when it takes a long period of time.

For illustrative purposes, again assume the Ibbotson rate, 9.2% per year, is the goal, which means essentially a doubling of capital over eight years. The required catchup rates become higher, obviously, with both the severity of the starting loss and the amount of time lost.

Table 2.3 Sustained Subsequent gains Needed to Recover Prior Losses		
Percent Lost at Beginning	Years until Loss Taken	Required Compound Return in Years Left, to Double in 8
10	1	12.1% for 7 years
	2	14.2 for 6
	3	17.3 for 5
	4	22.1 for 4
20	1	14.0%/yr for 7 years
	2	16.5 for 6
	3	20.1 for 5
	4	25.7 for 4
25	1	15.0%/yr for 7 years
	2	17.8 for 6
	3	21.7 for 5
	4	27.8 for 4
33.3	1	17.0%/yr for 7 years
	2	20.1 for 6
	3	24.6 for 5
	4	31.7 for 4
50	1	21.9%/yr for 7 years
	2	26.0 for 6
	3	32.0 for 5
	4	41.4 for 4

As Table 2.3 shows, taking a loss in the beginning requires that some pretty enviable returns be achieved to catch up to the doubling schedule in eight years. If you impose a higher desired return, such as perhaps 15%, the required catchup paces become breathtaking very quickly, even for fairly moderate losses. For example, the 15% rate triples money (3.059x) in eight years. Start out with a lazy 20% loss in the first 24 months, and the portfolio now must merely grow a little over 25% compounded for the final six years to attain 15% per year for the eight year period! Reaching for such rates will entail higher risk, so the endeavor will prove self-defeating for all but the most profoundly successful (or lucky) investors. To put that in context, the widely heralded Fidelity Magellan Fund under Peter Lynch achieved a return of 19.4% per annum from the end of 1983 to the middle of 1989 — some five and one-half years. That is a pretty lofty standard over an extended period, and one achieved with the help of a rising market that might not remain quite as helpful over the long term. What investor really can expect to gain 25% per year for six years especially in conservative retirement-oriented investment issues like utilities?

Another example may bring the reader up short (literally): suppose that at age 25 one invests $1,000 for retirement by 65, with the modest goal of the long-term 9.2% rate. If the money lies dormant for just the first year, the eventual retirement kitty will be depleted by $2,847. Worse yet, assume one suffers just a $200 loss (20%) in the first year and then gets the fund onto its 9.2% track: the final retirement fund will be short by $6,759 or by nearly 34 times the modest initial loss! This is why nonproductive investments, even in the conservative utilities area, must be summarily thrown overboard.

This chapter has been about *not losing* money. Now, having mulled over these thoughts, the reader should forever perceive a new, expanded, and more bitter meaning to the word loss. Keeping in mind what major long-term damage a small present loss can mean should help the investor focus on the straight-and-narrow path of conservative investing. Let others take the flyers. Pursue your target relentlessly and with single-minded devotion to your plan. Using utilities toward this end will keep the task simple and, executed in the manner described in coming chapters, will prove profitable over the long pull. There is enough potential profit available, with low risk, to make your program work.

So what if the strategy is a bit prosaic? So what if you don't have any I-can-top-that story of investment conquests to share on the train or at dinner parties? (Your neighbors never brag about their losses!). Smile knowingly. Ending up wealthy and without ulcers is the best revenge. The object of your program is profits rather than thrills; the key to profits is avoiding losses.

Time marches on: for you, or against you.

Finding Your Risk-Taking Level

What is the worst thing in life that could happen to you? Please, jot down your answer to that before you read on!

The four major arenas in which people fear loss are love, power, esteem, and money. If your answer to the question did not center on a financial loss, you have a typical attitude in this regard. If money worries shaped your response, you have an unusually strong aversion to financial risk and should take the warnings in this chapter very seriously. But even if your "worst thing" was not a money loss, you need to understand your feelings about financial risk so you will invest in ways that do not make you uncomfortable. Investments that you choose (in utilities or elsewhere) must be right for you not only in terms of objective but in terms of psychological tolerance.

This chapter is designed to help the reader define his or her own personal taste — or distaste — for risk. Each person is different. And each person must understand his or her personal emotional reactions to risk in order to have a realistic context for actions in realtime investment situations. A major objective is calibrating one's actions to one's risk tolerances so that the investment program remains comfortable and does not become a source of personal tension. Bernard Baruch, the legendary investor, is reputed to have advised to "invest only up to the sleeping point." Each of us has our own trigger level for insomnia.

In reading the next several pages, think of risk not merely in terms of the likelihood and degree of any possible loss, but also as a measure of the uncertainty of just how positive your gain or return will actually be. It is critically important for new utilities investors (I think of you as "CD refugees") to understand that even in the shelter of the relatively predictable utilities industry the stock and bond markets are quite unlike certificates of deposit. There is no guaranty of a certain return, and there definitely will be fluctuation on the way to the end. Understanding this aspect of risk and discovering your personal capacity to function in an environment of financial uncertainty are required for your investment success.

In this chapter several games of chance will be described. In each, you will be asked to decide how far up the scale of risk you would be comfortable in still playing, and when it would be time to quit. As a preface, it will be useful for some readers to have a brief review of very elementary concepts in probability and statistics as they pertain to games of chance. (Those highly familiar with probability theory can safely skip ahead to the actual risk-testing questions.) In particular, we need to focus on the so-called "value of an event."

> The net expected value of an event is the sum of the
> products of the individual outcomes' values times
> their probabilities.

For example, imagine the flipping of a fair coin. If Mary wins $1 from John for heads but loses $1 to John for tails, the net value of the game to each person is zero. This is because each event has a 50% probability of occurring and one has a negative value equal to the positive value of the other. For Mary, the results are as follows:

Event	Probability	Outcome	Net Value
Heads	.5	win $1.00	+$0.50
Tails	.5	lose $1.00	- $0.50
Net Expected Value of the Game (i.e, the sum)			$0.00

Organized gambling games—whether legalized or not — have a net negative value to the player and a net positive value to the organizer. For example, over the long term a casino will, on average, win a small percentage of the total amount bet. That is because the payoffs of wins times the probability of those wins for guests add up to less than 100% of the total amount wagered. In other words, the value of the game is negative to the bettors and positive to the house. Similarly, in a state lottery, the players win back about 40 to 45% of the total played; the rest goes to administration and social expenditures. This is a highly negative-value game, but people play — generally in small amounts — because of the attraction of the possible big payoff. Most casino games provide the player with better odds than does the lottery.

Game # 1: How Much of an Odds-On Bet Would You Make?

To introduce the idea of risk tolerances, imagine this game. You are invited by a casino to play once and only once the following game (suppose they have a sure way to prevent you from playing more than once): There will be one and only one flip of a fair coin. You will call the toss. If you are correct, you will win two dollars. If you are wrong, you will lose one dollar. (All the money will be deposited in advance with a trustworthy neutral party who will make the payoff to the winner—either you or the casino—immediately after the flip.) Do you wish to play?

> The expected value of this game to the invited
> player is a positive $0.50. There is a 50% chance
> of winning $2, less a 50% chance of losing $1.00;
> the net value is $1.00 less $0.50 or a positive $0.50.

Almost anyone (assuming they are not morally opposed to gambling and not desperately poor) would willingly take the chance. The catch, of course, is that there is to be only one play, so there is no "in the long run" effect that would work in favor of the player. One flip only. Win or lose. End of game.

Would you play $1 for the chance to win $2?

Or $5 for the chance to win $10?

How about $20 for the chance to win $40?

Would you play $50 for the chance to win $100?

But would you risk $250 for the chance to win $500?

Or $500 for the chance to win $1,000?

Would you play $1,000 for the chance to win $2,000?

Would you ante up $5,000 for the chance to win $10,000?

. . . and so on?

Where Would You Stop?

Each person has his or her own stopping point. There is no "correct" answer. (Actually, since the game has a positive expected value to the invited player, it would be rational to play rather than to refuse, so playing some amount is the "correct" response.) But each person has his or her own risk tolerance. The stopping point is determined by several factors:

- Total personal wealth
- Total financial responsibilities and contingencies
- Source of funds (winnings versus hard earned)
- Cash immediately on hand
- Nature and timing of other opportunities
- Prospective cash flow
- Expected timing of cash flow
- Tax buffering, if any, of gain or loss
- Tendency to "feel lucky"
- Pleasure at winning versus pain upon losing
- Identity of winner if you lose (e.g., charity or friend versus casino)

Again, each reader will choose his or her own "sleeping point" on this game. While the specific point where each reader says "no, thanks" is not especially important, the reasons underlying the decision are. They should be understood. Two people of equal wealth and age may decide differently because they have different income prospects and/or varying financial responsibilities. Two people of identical financial resources, income levels, and needs may have different responses because their ages differ, so the time required to recoup loss has different meaning. And so on. Or—and this is very important—even aside from the logic and the purely financial aspects of a given game, some people simply like to play more than others, and some people feel very great pain incurring any loss.

Examine the reasons you decided to stop at some point. Suppose you would play $500 for the chance to win twice that, but would not put up $1,000 for a chance at $2,000. Why? You know that the "logical" or rational choice is to play since it is a positive-value game. What stops you? Your income level? Your age and the thought of possibly losing too much to tolerate? The fact your spouse would know? Your near-term financial obligations such as a mortgage or tuition? The "other things you could do with the money" if you did not play? Just the pain of losing at all? Understand what makes you tick. This will help you to define your risk tolerance. Write down your reasons. Save them for future reference. The risk-tolerance "personality" you document will help to define investment options that will make you comfortable and uncomfortable.

Game #2: How Much Variance in Outcomes Will You Accept?

In this game, there will again be a positive net expected value, but the range of possible outcomes will be varied. Two coins will be flipped. If both are heads, the most positive payoff will occur. If both are tails, the most negative payoff will apply. If there is a mix (one head and one tail), the middle-value payoff will occur. The odds are as follows:

Clearly, as long as the difference between high and middle value

Outcome	Coin1/Coin2		Payoff	Odds	Value	Cash Value
#1	H	H	High	.25	0.25x high value	+$2.00
#2	H	T	Mid	.25	0.25x mid value	+$1.00
#3	T	H	Mid	.25	0.25x mid value	+$1.00
#4	T	T	Low	.25	0.25x low value	$0.00

equals the difference between middle and low value, the net value of the game is the middle-value. For example, suppose the payoff values were to be $2, $1 and zero, as shown in the table above. The net value of the game would be a positive $1. Would you play that game? Virtually anyone would, if there were no entry fee. Logically, one "should" be willing to play for any entry fee up to a dollar, because the "value" of the game to the player is equal to that amount. But some people are so averse to risk that they would refuse to play if there were any chance they could come out a net loser. Their reasons may be financial (can't afford to lose) or psychological (can't stand losing) or some combination of the two. Everyone's reasons will vary. No reasons are "wrong."

Some people would play the above game, even with some chance of a net loss, but only up to a certain tolerable amount. People who would refuse to play if there is any chance of loss have the mindset of the lifelong CD investor: the returns may be low, but they are predictable and there is no chance (or, so they think!) of loss. If you find in studying the various examples in this chapter that you are very uncomfortable with possibly suffering a loss, investing in the stock or bond market, either directly or through mutual funds, is going to be too scary for you. In your mind you want the higher returns and you say you can live with the risk, but in your gut you will develop ulcers when a loss occurs. A caution: while investing in utilities is a lower-risk approach —and historically a higher-return approach—to the stock market than most others, it is not without risk. You have no control over events. You may be able to quit the game with just a small loss, but you cannot turn back the clock and get all your money returned in the stock and bond markets, including in the utilities area. If you invest $5,000 in 200 shares of a gas or telephone company's stock (or any other kind, for that matter), you no longer have $5,000. You have 200 shares of stock whose market value will continue to change daily.

Now consider some more examples of financial games.

Game #3. Even Wider Variation in Outcomes

Again, as in game #1, the payoff is secured by a neutral agent, so fraud is not an issue. Suppose there are three sealed envelopes, and you can choose one and only one. Each envelope contains an insured bank's certificate of deposit for $1,000, with an absolutely unbreakable one-year term. But each CD has a different interest rate. Suppose those interest rates (as in the "good old days") are 6%, 8%, and 10%. Would you pay $1,000 for the chance to draw one of the three CDs blindly? Would you play the game if the best available rate on one-year CDs otherwise were only 7.5%? Or only if the going rate were even lower? (This example must be viewed in context of the prevailing rates at the time of reading, of course.)

Clearly, the value of this game is an expected 8% return, but the outcome could be as good as 10% or as bad as 6%. Given the opportunity cost of a 7.5% rate (or perhaps some lower rate), many investors would play, but others would find the chance of losing, i.e., getting only 6% for a year, unacceptable. If the envelopes contained five-year CDs, more people would probably avoid playing, since being (and feeling) stuck for five years with the below-market rate would be too painful.

Game #4: Same Net Value; Lower Odds of Relative Disappointment

There can be variants applied, with the net expected value still held constant at 8%. For example, there could be ten envelopes: eight with 8% CDs, one with a 6% CD, and one with the juicy 10% CD hidden inside. Now the odds of not losing are much higher (nine out of ten), while the expected value is still the same 8%. Probably many more investors would play. But again, personal factors would determine each investor's decision. If the size of the CD were $5,000 or $10,000 or $25,000, the population willing to play would decrease somewhat since the 6% result would be a major opportunity loss.

Game #5: Wide Range of Outcomes, Including Actual Loss

Now suppose that while the expected return remains constant, the range of possible outcomes is widened. With three envelopes, suppose the CDs are for 8%, 13%, and just 3%. Would you play the game? Would you be more willing to play if the range of payoffs were narrower, say at 8%, 5%, and 11%? Or if you have a certain gambler's streak, would you play if the outcomes were 8%, 16%, and zero? Actual surveys indicate that a significant percentage of people would play this latter game for a modest-sized investment of, say, $1,000 for one year. But as the unbreakable terms are longer and/or the minimum-size certificate is increased, more people decline to play.

What if the payoffs were to be 8%, 20%, and minus 4%? Would you take the chance of a 4% loss of capital for the chance of a windfall 20% rate? Surveys indicate that a significant barrier comes into play when any possible actual loss is introduced. The barrier is much more noticeable than the mere opportunity-loss barrier of getting less than the 7.5% one could get from the bank without taking the game's chances. What if there were, again, ten envelopes: eight at 8%, one at 20%, and one at minus 4%. Would that make you more willing to play, with only a 10% chance of really losing? Perhaps. Again, there is no "correct" answer, but there is an answer most comfortable for you. And no doubt your response would change as the term or the minimum dollar amount got larger.

Think about how you reacted to this latest proposed game. Analyze what made you say "no" at a certain point. Write down your thinking; save it for future reference.

Game #6: Will You Play a Skewed Game?

Let us continue to suppose you are investing in CDs at First Federal Venturesome Savers' Bank and Trust. Now assume the rolling of an honest pair of dice. Just one roll! Snake eyes gives you a zero return on a one year, $1,000 CD. Any roll from 3 to 11 gives you 8.15% on your money. Double 6s gives you 11%. In this game, the expected payoff is 34/36 times 8.15%, plus 1/36 times 11%, plus 1/36 times zero, for an actual expected value of

8%. But even though most players will get 8.15%, the possible results are skewed to the downside. You have one chance of winning a little more (11% vs. just 8.15%) but an equal although small chance of losing a lot more (by getting snake eyes for a zero return rather than 8.15%). Relatively few people would play this game if the available certain return on a normal CD were 8% — even knowing there are 35 of 36 chances they will come out ahead by earning 8.15% or better. If you would play this game, you are unusually comfortable with taking risks.

Now suppose that the range of results were set up to be even wider, with a greater positive reward at one end but a negative return at the other; for example if the top return were 16% and the snake-eyes result a negative 5%. The expected value is the same. Would you play? Suppose the outlying results were +26% and -15%. Do you begin to see how you feel about different kinds of risk, and in particular how you feel about taking a loss? This is an important self-insight since investing in utilities is *not* a guaranteed-win situation even though it is an expected-win opportunity over the long term.

Game #7: A Positive Skew

Suppose the skewing went the other way. Suppose snake eyes gets 4%, rolls of 3 to 11 get 7.9%, and double sixes pay off with a handsome 15.5% return. Here, the probabilities add to the familiar 8% expected rate, but the downside is not as severe losing as the upside reward. But in return for that less painful worse case, you get a most likely 7.9% return, not 8.15% or even 8%. Would you play? Or would you settle for a sure 8%? Would you prefer this game to #6? If so, you will like investments that produce a lower return in exchange for greater assurance of a less drastic downside. Of course, in investing you must realize that there is no actual assurance of what the downside will be. One can draw scenarios to imagine the limits, and one can place stop orders, but there really are no actual iron-clad guarantees. If you do not like that reality, CDs are the place for you.

Now again look again at Game #7 but suppose that the range of results were set up to be even wider, with a greater positive reward at one end but a correspondingly more negative outcome at the other. Would you play? If you would, would you be inclined to risk only a smaller amount of money on this game? Again, think about how you reacted to this latest proposed game. Analyze what made you like or dislike the various versions. Write down your self-analysis for future reference.

Investing randomly in even fairly conservative instruments such as utility securities (especially their common stocks) is quite like the downside-skewed Game #6. Chosen randomly, most utility common stocks would produce returns (at least in the short term) that bunch together near the mean. There might be a few that give moderate positive surprises. But a few will produce nasty downside results, including more than tiny losses of capital. (Chapter 11 is devoted to identifying, for weeding out, those specific stocks most likely to produce losses; the selection and timing system developed in this book, especially in Chapter 14, tends to produce above-average results by weeding out the likely nasty surprises, so the investor can participate in a game that is better than merely random! But no investment system guarantees against loss.)

Note: games #2 through #7 were stated as single-chance situations: you may play only once or else pass. Suppose these games allowed you to play three or six times each rather than once. Now are you much more inclined to play? If so, you will find it important to diversify your investments rather than placing too much into any one basket. And you will feel that such diversification provides a cushion that makes the taking of risk more acceptable. If the idea of three or six plays rather than one did not influence your attraction to the games, you exhibit a pretty strong aversion to risk even in situations where the odds favor a win: you really have a hard time with any chance at all of taking a loss.

Game #8: If You Knew the Result, Could You Tolerate the Ride?

Yet another test of your comfort with, or aversion to, risk centers on the likelihood of consistent profit. Suppose that you are presented a game, or investment, whose long-term expected rate of return is 10% per year. Suppose that you find that rate acceptable and really believe it will be delivered, based on good evidence from past experience. Suppose that the game must be played for 20 years or not at all. The only catch is that the 10% "average" or expected rate will not occur in any single year, nor will the average 10% compounded result be available at any time except at the end. Rates will vary sharply, from plus 25% to minus 25%, in any given year. But on average, over the long term, the net compounded rate will be a positive 10%. Will you invest?

Suppose there will be only one year in 20 when there is a loss of capital. Could you tolerate that ride? Suppose there were to be five bad years, when money is lost, out of the 20? Would you still invest? Suppose 40% of the years, or eight out of 20, were to produce negative results, but the net outcome in the long run would end up as plus 10% per year. Could you tolerate that rollercoaster ride? There is no one correct answer. Suppose there might be as many as 3 losing years in a row—enough to really shake your confidence while CDs provide double digit returns! Do you think you would have the guts to ride it out? How sure are you? In theory, an average of 10% compounded (as from the market) is just that: an average but not a point-to-point guarantee. It's a whole lot different than a *sure* 10% every year (as in CDs). And some investors could not stand the emotional jostling along the way.

Can you?

Again, think about how you reacted to the various possibilities in the games above, especially Game #8. What made you like or dislike the various versions of the games? Write down your thoughts for future reference. They will help you understand your own risk profile. And that knowledge is important to executing a successful investment program.

Game #9: Las Vegas

Have you ever gone to Las Vegas, Monte Carlo, Atlantic City, or another spot where gambling is a big-time activity? Did you play? Did you set a limit? Did you adhere to it? What kinds of games did you find that you like: games of total chance such as roulette or craps, or other games such as poker or blackjack, where skill plays a part, giving you more control over the situation? If you won a sweepstakes in which you had the choice of a gambling/resort destination and some other vacation of equal value, time, and distance, and assuming you had never been to either one, which would you choose?   Again, there is no "correct" attitude, but understanding your reactions to such choices in advance will be very useful in helping you understand your own attitudes toward investing.

Many books have been written about the psychology of gambling; you may wish to read one or more to understand more deeply the way you feel about taking financial risks (the reading list in Appendix II) includes two books on the psychology of investing.   Other books are available on the general subject of taking risks outside a financial context. There are many psychological aspects of taking chances, and for the serious reader or the serious student of human nature such subjects are also worth the time invested.   According to many authorities on psychology, willingness to take risk in one aspect of life (water skiing, or choosing a life partner, for example), is not necessarily correlated with one's attraction to financial risks. Just because people call you a daredevil in the great outdoors does not mean you will be able to handle a financial loss casually.   Get to know yourself as best you can.

Game #10. Double or Nothing

Go back, mentally, to coin flipping. Suppose you are in a voluntary sequence-type 50/50 random game in which the required bet is double or nothing at each step. Suppose you have won several rounds in a row, starting at $1, and now you are at $16. When will you quit? Will you go to $32, to $64, to $128, or even higher? Suppose the minimum ante were $10 to start and you were at the $160-ahead level. Would you go to $320 (or nothing), to $640, or to $1,280? Would your answer be any different, do you suppose, if the original stake (the $1 or $10, or whatever) had been a gift rather than something brought to the table from your paycheck? Would your tendency to keep playing versus your likelihood of quitting be different if the successive flips were scheduled one week apart instead of within the next 30 seconds each time? What if your spouse or your neighbors or your boss were watching? Would that change your behavior? What if you were a contestant on a national TV game show. . . would that influence just how far out on the limb you'd venture? Think about these things, and figure out what influences your willingness to take risk, or your need to avoid it.

Now, think about the downside for a minute. Suppose you started flipping coins on a bet and were losing, with the starting ante at $1 (or $10). Suppose you were now down by $16, or $40, or $160! And suppose there were a small chance, based on some uncontrollable event, that the game could come to a permanent end while you were behind, forcing to you pay off your loss without another chance to go double or nothing to erase your self-imposed debt. This sounds a little unnerving, doesn't it? How deep in the hole would you go before voluntarily stopping, lest you lose "just one more round" and find the game abruptly ended? Your feelings on this kind of a game will help you to understand how you feel about losses in several ways: in relation to chance or "cruel fate;" in relation to your overall wealth and income stream; and in relation to your sense of control over a situation. Again, make a few written notes about your innermost financial self.

Game #11. The Track

Have you ever gone to the races? If yes, did you enjoy the experience? If not, would you like to go? Would/did you go alone, or with someone? Would/did you vow just to observe the first time, betting no money? Would/did you set a firm limit on how much to risk? Would you carry more money than your limit and be able to keep some in your pocket if you lost your limit? What kind of bettor are you: do you bet the combinations or underdogs for the long shot with a huge payoff? Do you prefer to play the odds-on favorite to win, looking for a bunch of moderate net wins but risking loss if the favorites fail? Do you play the favorites to place or to show? Do you feel in control when betting because you have studied the racing form for past patterns? Or do you think it's just as good an idea to bet the names or colors that strike your fancy? Do you like betting on races more than wagering in the state lottery? Do you have a nagging suspicion (no pun intended, really) that maybe the whole racing game is fixed? Your attitudes on this series of questions will again help you to understand your tolerance/taste for taking risks and your pattern of comfort or discomfort as to specific different types of risk. The more control you prefer, the less likely you are to be comfortable using mutual funds to invest in utilities (or elsewhere).

Game #12. The World Series Pool

Does your work place have a pool most years? (If you happen to be the organizer, give yourself 10 extra points as a lover of risk!) Suppose someone else sets up the game but you (secretly) are allowed to set the bet that all players will contribute. Do you say $1, $5, $10, or what? What kinds of pools do you like best: winner takes all? Separate winners on each game and a bigger winner at the end? Do you like to be able to choose your favorite home/visitor half inning, or do you just equally enjoy a random selection in which your winning score is drawn from a hat? Would you really rather give or get a certain number of runs for the series and bet your team win/lose with a single friend instead of going into the pool? Or frankly, do you wish there were no pool so you would not feel forced to join in the supposed "fun" at all?

Here again, your attitudes will tip you off to issues like control, privacy, crowd psychology, and peer pressure, and high versus low stakes. Those attitudes will help you to understand yourself in relation to your investments.

Game #13: The Sudden Trust Fund

Suppose you suddenly become beneficiary of a $100,000 trust fund which you must invest for a 10-year minimum period before receiving any cash to use. How much of the money will you invest aggressively, exposing it to significant risk in the pursuit of possible extraordinary gain? How much will you keep in CDs "to avoid any chance of losing it"? Will you put all the money in one kind of investment or spread it around over several? Your answers will help you understand your attitude toward gains and losses. In particular, pay attention to your first instinct on how much you will put at serious risk. Also, notice whether the wind-fall source of the fund prompts you to feel or behave differently than if you had earned and accumulated the money, as would be the case if you receive a rollover distribution from a former employer's retirement plan.

Game #14: The Principal-Returned Trust Fund

Now suppose this $100,000 trust fund comes with one long string attached: at the end of the 10 years, you must return the $100,000 starting sum to the trust grantor and can keep any net increase you have created *but must make up any net losses you might sustain.* Does that change your intended investment mix? For most people, it implies a more conservative approach. If your investment approach would be little changed, this implies you have strong confidence in your abilities and in your Game #13 choices.

Game #15: The No-Recourse Trust Fund

Finally, suppose the $100,000 trust comes with a slightly different twist: you can keep any gains above the starting principal and must return the $100,000 if you have a net profit—but if you have a net loss, you simply return everything that's left. In effect, you have no risk of loss but can keep all your gains. Clearly, most people would greatly prefer this to the prior situation wherein $100,000 must definitely be returned. But does this game invite you to invest more aggressively? If not, you are reacting to a psychological aversion to uncertainty, since your actual monetary risk is zero. Your only true potential "loss" is the potential of gains missed.

CONCLUSION

Each reader will have developed a sense of his or her own taste or distaste for risk by following the games, questions, and commentary in this chapter. As a result, each will now better understand the kinds of investment situations that should be avoided. For some, most risks will be truly tolerable. An occasional loss will be regretted but will not cause interminable agony. For others, taking just about any possible steps to avoid a loss will be preferred, even if this approach means accepting a lower expected rate of return (or value of the game). The profile each investor discovers will determine such things as the appropriateness of stocks versus bonds, and the choice of short-versus long-term bonds in a utility portfolio.

One other particularly interesting aspect of the acceptance of risk and the possibility of resulting gain or loss is tied to ego. For some people, participation and control in the chance situation are important. Would you play the state lottery only if you could choose your numbers, or would you let a computer select them for you? Do you prefer random casino games such as roulette or slot machines, or instead blackjack or poker, where the player has control over when to play or fold, thus exerting nonrandom influence over the odds? Your answers to questions such as these will indicate the degree to which you will want to participate in managing your own money. The answers are also strongly related to your willingness to take responsibility for your own decisions.

Investors who wish active participation will prefer to select individual securities for themselves. Those content to allow the long-term odds to work without their personal intervention will find a managed investment account such as a mutual fund better suited to their tastes. Chapter 25 covers that alternative, for those who like it. Specific open-end and closed-end funds that invest in utilities will be named.

 The purpose of this chapter has been for the reader to gain self-understanding regarding risk tolerance/aversion. This individualized information is critical to developing a workable investment program—in utilities or any other media. Without a solid understanding of one's own reaction to risk and loss—and to gain as well—the investor will react sharply to events and will probably swing from one pole to the other emotionally. Such swings will be reflected in irrational and extreme investment actions like buying in the euphoria near a top and/or panicking and selling it all near the bottom — which will prove self defeating and extremely costly. Self-knowledge is power; lack of it is very dangerous to your financial health.

One important caveat: this chapter has discussed mathematical odds and has invited the reader to decide what sorts of games are comfortable. In the real arena of investing, the actual odds are never fully known when decisions are made. And even if one roughly estimates the returns before entering the game, the probabilities will continue to change once a portfolio is already owned. Good situations can gradually or swiftly become bad situations, and vice versa. Therefore one is always dealing in greater uncertainty than has been explored in the preceding pages. The investment process is of its nature supported by optimism (else all funds would be buried in basements and back yards). For that reason, the rational investor should assume that the real odds of success—or the truly likely returns— are lower than he or she actually perceives. The eventual outcome of any investment is a single, discrete result, so percentages of likely success or estimated expected results are academic and, many would say, meaningless in retrospect. By definition, the result is likely to be better or worse than the "expected" computed outcome. Therefore it is especially important for the conservative, serious investor to err on the side of caution in accepting a risk-bearing posture.

One further caveat: prospectuses and advertisements for mutual funds caution the investor that "past results do not in any way guarantee future performance." This is literally true, and must be accepted by investors not only in funds but even more so in individual stocks. In utilities investing, there is a subtle and very dangerous tendency to rely on the evidence of past fundamentals (for example, the dividend that's been paid for 80 years in a row); long strings of positive feedback give the investor a sense of comfort sometimes greater than new realities will justify. Next year's or next quarter's dividend will be determined by future events, not by a string of ancient-history successes. The investor must develop the attitude that change rather than permanency is the expected norm, and must have the discipline to switch investment positions whenever such action is indicated. Long-term investing is not never-sell investing. And a conservative strategy and the comfort of past dividend income must not be allowed to beguile the investor into ill-founded optimism or complacency. All income investments other than short-term T-bills, insured CDs, and insured bank accounts entail a risk to capital by offering potentially unknown—although apparently attractive—

income streams. To face uncertainty, investors must be psychologically prepared. Investor, know thyself![1]

1. In November 1992, both Fidelity Investments and The Dreyfus Corporation announced they were developing questionnaires that would enable their sales representatives and individual investors to establish desired risk tolerances. These documents were still unavailable at publication time. But if they truly probe more deeply than asking investors to rate themselves arbitrarily on scales of risk acceptance or to state preferences of types of investment media, they represent breakthroughs well worth pursuing. In the past, brokerage agreements have requested simple categories checked off by the investor, and the results have been used mainly for legal defense of the broker rather than primarily to help the investor choose appropriate investments.

Defining Your Target Rate of Return

Probably the most widely cited study of long-term stock-market performance, as mentioned in Chapter 2, is that by Roger Ibbotson and Rex Sinquefield, *Stocks, Bonds, Bills, and Inflation: the Past (1926-1976) and the Future (1977-2000)*. This study showed that over a very long period of time (and even in 10-year periods) common stocks provide higher average returns than the other investment media covered. In fact, the all-important "magic number" for common stocks was 9.2% per annum. That return included both capital appreciation and dividends. According to *SBBI, 1992 Yearbook*, by Ibbotson Associates (Chicago), the strong markets since 1981 raised the overall average for the 65-year period 1926-1991 to 10.4%. After some less-strong future years are added on, the benchmark will probably subside to somewhere in the 9% to 10% range. The 1980s saw significant reductions in both corporate and personal tax rates as well as about a 50% retreat from the record-high interest rates of the Carter presidency. Such bullish drivers will not be repeated from the present starting point. So investment returns cannot be expected to continue at 1980s' rates.

Now 9% or 10% may not sound exciting in light of the inflation rate we endured from the late 1960s to the middle 1980s, or in context of the rapid increase in the Dow Jones Industrial Average that began in 1982. But keep your longer-term perspective: expect that the high recent equity-return rates will prove exceptions rather than the rule when we look back. This caution on expectations was expressed by the highly regarded Warren Buffett in his essay to investors in the 1992 annual report of Berkshire

Hathaway. And remember, too, that as a utilities investor you are seeking financial return rather than excitement.

The 9.2% or 10.4% rule of thumb can be a useful starting point for evaluating reasonable long-term returns. Aggressive equities investors should aim for higher returns, probably on the order of 15% or more per year, as compensation for the intellectual work and emotional energy expended in owning stocks. But a 9% or 10% standard is historically unassailable as the demonstrated average, and is useful for making a key point about the time value of money.

Let us again look at the table illustrating the so-called Rule of 72, which easily tells how long it takes to double a sum of money at annual compounded rates. For example, 7.2% for 10 years, compounded annually, produces $2,004.22 from an original $1,000 investment. Table 4.1 provides the actual numbers. There are three formulations of the Rule of 72:

- Years times rate equals (pretty nearly) 72, or

- 72 divided by rate equals number of years required; or

- 72 divided by available years equals rate required to double a sum.

Table 4.1 The Rule of 72 in Action			
Years	Rule-Implied Rate in %	Multiple of Starting Sum	Actual Rate to Double
3	24	1.907	26%
4	18	1.939	18.9
5	14.4	1.959	14.9
6	12	1.974	12.25
7	10.3	1.986	10.4
8	9	1.993	9.05
9	8	1.999	8
10	7.2	2.004	7.2
11	6.5	1.999	6.5
12	6	2.012	5.95
13	5.5	2.006	5.5
14	5.1	2.006	5.1

The table has been truncated at 14 years because the returns at that point decline to below typical savings passbook or T-bill rates (at least until those of the early 1990s!), which are wholly unacceptable returns for those assuming the risks of equity ownership.

The table may provide useful information for planning purposes for investors looking ahead to retirement, college expenses, and other major financial requirements. Note that this table represents sums of money compounding smoothly as if in a long-term CD or a zero-coupon bond. The actual experience that a utility bond or equity investor will have will never represent such a smooth path. There will be ups and downs along the way as interest rates fluctuate.

Averages, of course, are statistical or mathematical artifacts and can be misleading. There is, especially in investments, a wide dispersion of results around the mathematical mean or median. Some "investments" go to zero, and a few others multiply several-fold, even in short periods such as a year or less. Throughout this book the importance of preventing losses will be stressed. The reason is that after time and money are lost the investor must pursue a more risky strategy to regain the losses and eventually arrive at the goal. And higher risk can lead to further losses, digging the hole even deeper.

ADVANTAGES OF DIVIDEND-PAYING STOCKS

As one might suspect, the variation in price performance among stocks that pay dividends tends to be less extreme than among those that do not. Three recent periods of relatively flat stock prices confirmed this: the second halves of calendar 1988, 1989, and 1991. Using the Value Line universe of 1,600 stocks (which in itself screens out large number of speculative, low-capitalization, and low-priced stocks, thereby understating the true extent of variability of price volatility in the overall market), it is apparent from Table 4.2 that dividend-paying issues generally and utilities specifically showed more predictable (i.e., less variable) performance (as well as better net results) in these roughly "sideways" market periods. Similar studies for periods of greater net market movement would show utilities' prices to be more stable (in both up and down markets) and to have lower standard deviation of result as well. Utilities may not provide excitement . . . but that is precisely in line with the conservative investor's goal.

Table 4.2 Effect of Dividends on Stocks' Returns and Dispersion of Returns			
	Number	Price Chg.	Std Dev.
1988 Second Half			
Non-Dividend Payers	389	-6.1%	25.5%
Dividend Payers	1201	-0.7%	15.4%
Utilities	182	+2.9%	13.3%
Utilities with Dividends	165	+2.5%	11.6%
1989 Second Half			
Non-Dividend Payers	393	-8.6%	29.6%
Dividend Payers	1200	+1.6%	18.7%
Utilities	183	+8.8%	10.9%
Utilities with Dividends	165	+10.2%	9.0%
1991 Second Half			
Non-Dividend Payers	408	+8.7%	36.4%
Dividend Payers	1193	+9.9%	23.5%
Utilities	189	+11.7%	18.7%
Utilities with Dividends	169	+13.9%	14.3%

In the sideways periods of 1988 and 1989, utility shares outperformed others on average by between 3% and 7%—before adding in the advantage of higher dividend income. Even in the last half of 1991, which included a late upward price slope, utility shares gained more in price than others. This relatively small time sampling, however, should not set the standards for expected performance, nor should the strong action in the market averages since 1982, driven mainly by falling interest rates.

A standard comparing utilities to the overall market, factoring in the obvious positive difference in yield, seems appropriate. Using this measure, average utility stocks in recent years have provided cash yields of about 3% or 4% per year above those of the broad stock market as a whole. Thus, utilities, by paying more cash return on average, have an advantage in terms of the yield component of possible total return. Adding about 3% or 4% for extra dividend yields to the Ibbotson common-equity returns of 9.2% (1977) or 10.4% (1992) produces a target of about a 13% average per annum. This total average annual target return for utility investing, using the Rule of 72, implies that money would virtually double every 5.5 years on average and would quadruple in 11 years. How many investors who have followed a more speculative course can claim such good long-term results?

What most investors would never guess is that, over long periods of time, investing in utility stocks actually has produced a slightly higher rate of return than investing in major industrial stocks, such as those in the DJIA or the S&P 500. The difference, according to a study done by Shearson Lehman Brothers in late 1992, is a bit under 1% per year in favor of utility stocks. Two points are important in putting this into context. First, as shown in Table 4.2, variability of returns on utilities is lower (that's good!). And second, the system developed in this book is designed to *provide utility-stock returns in excess of the average,* by both avoiding losses and selecting high *total-return* stocks.

Another look at history suggests that utilities investing should return at least as much as that in the overall market. Using the Standard & Poor's Utilities Index, and duplicating the 50-year period of the original Ibbotson study, the result for utilities was an average total return of 9.5% per year, with 35 winning years in 50. This performance was achieved despite some dismal performances in the depression years. Beginning in the present era wherein utility shares sell at a higher yield than the general market, one can reasonably expect a higher total return — and less downside risk — when starting with the utilities' extra 3% or 4% in cash return as compared with the general market.

Arguably, the utilities investor well might adopt a premium-performance expectation, given that utility investing involves dividend payers, which as a group tend to outperform the market. Since the selection criteria developed later in this book are designed to generate positive performance by avoiding losses, some investors may indeed be comfortable with a higher goal than 13% per year. Since no quantitative increment can be defined or supported by empirical evidence, however, I advise a long-term target 13% rate. Be aware that achieving this in the short term may be difficult when one starts with the low yields of the early 1990s.

CONCLUSION

It is important that an investment program be grounded on reasonable expectations, and that the investor truly accept the realities of what the likely returns are. If expectations are unrealistic, at some point the investor will abandon the program in favor of the lure of "hot ideas" and short-term appreciation. Such changes of approach almost always prove disastrous for the conservative investor, not least because they are usually undertaken in an already high market (when optimism is high and profits are visible all around) rather than at the bottom of a bear cycle when potentials are actually greatest.

Another temptation against which the investor is strongly cautioned: *do not seek the highest possible cash return from utilities,* since clear evidence indicates this involves high risk and therefore danger to your capital as well as your income stream. Although utilities do provide the inherent advantage of a higher cash yield than the broad market, seeking to capture as much as possible of the overall investment-return goal in the form of cash return is, ironically, a mistake. Instead, as I will advise in Chapter 13, seek total return.

Understand what a reasonable goal is—over the long term—when investing in utilities, and accept that return as your standard. A long-term average in the range of 10% to 13% per year should be attainable for investors who are disciplined and who apply the selection principles to be laid out in later chapters.

Why This Plan Will Work for You

In any business or investment venture, it is very important to assess—before starting—the chances for success. One must be realistic. Whether building a house (will you run out of money before finishing?) or starting a business (do you know the market and the competition?) or inventing a new gizmo (do you understand the technology and the economics involved?), one should always take a serious look at the terrain before charging ahead. Fortunately, investing in utilities presents the average non-professional investor a relatively uncommon favorable combination of key factors allowing a very good chance for success.

FACTORS DRIVING INVESTOR FAILURE

To show how and why a disciplined and intelligent program of investing in utilities can be successful for you, it is useful to look first at the factors for investment failure. Once these are understood, one can see fairly easily, by contrast, that the utilities area offers the potential for success. Here, then, are six factors that all too often lead to investment disaster for the investor:

- Unsound fundamentals: The industry or technology is in decline, is not truly essential, is in legal jeopardy, or may become technologically displaced.

- Incomprehensibility: The area is beyond the capacity of most mortals to understand; it is suited only to "rocket scientists" and/or requires huge time investment.

- Hype and Novelty: The investment concept is characterized by hype and promotion; brokers, underwriters, and the press are likely to tout prospects of getting rich quickly; the industry or technology is so new that it is both exciting and untested.

- High Drama and Emotion: Developments have major shock value in the news, leading the crowd to herd-like behavior and likely swaying the investor to act on emotional rather than purely logical considerations.

- Lack of Structure or System: Because of complexity, lack of sufficient data, and/or lack of a discernible pattern, there is no reasonable and understandable basis for creating a system which, if followed consistently, would help the investor achieve success.

- Investor Irrationality: The type of investor typically attracted to certain types of investments is prone to undisciplined, illogical, and erratic behavior and thus is probably "doomed from the start" to fail; the expectations are economically impossible to reach.

THE GOOD NEWS: UTILITIES INVESTING PRESENTS FACTORS FOR SUCCESS

Investing in utilities for capital preservation, growth, and income presents a most unusual combination of factors that do not fall into the above-described formula for investment failure. As you move further through the book to explore the system presented, it will be useful to have in mind the positive elements present, the factors that are on your side rather than conspiring against you.

Investing in utilities presents the following favorable aspects which, in combination, add to the potential for success:
- Fundamentals are solid for the long term.
- This is basically an understandable industry (or group of industries) which the lay person can relate to.
- There is a lack of hype or novelty.
- The content is unexciting, unemotional.
- Significant information and a systematic approach are readily available.
- You are a relatively mature and reasonable investor, not an emotion-driven, high-stakes gambler.

Fundamentals on your side. It is comforting to the utilities investor to realize the very high probability that the industry will endure though time. We cannot conceive of civilized society in which we do not have heat and power, communications, or water. Short of a nuclear holocaust that devours modern economic society and makes any book on investing highly moot, it is likely that we will continue to use electric power, natural gas, and telephone communications. Our lives physically depend on water as well. Displacement of energy (electric power and gas) utilities would require the invention of a magical source of energy, which physics and the other sciences tell us is impossible: the perpetual-motion machine or some other "free" source of energy whose output exceeds its input. The closest we seemingly will come to such a dream are solar power and nuclear fusion technologies.

But both of these are highly capital intensive, implying that a public utility vehicle is the means of choice for assembling the necessary pieces and distributing the power to the user. If we assume continuance of a capitalist society—and worldwide political developments in recent years show that the tide is flowing out for command economies not based on individual incentive—then one can take comfort in investing in privately owned utility enterprises: the technology is essential, the demand seems insatiable, and the capital investment is so huge that expropriation seems impossible in a free society.

Understandability. Fortunately, the utilities industry is not a "rocket-science" challenge for the lay investor to understand. Demand factors are apparent; regulation is a public matter of record whose process and rules are well established; the operating and financial economics of the business are pretty basic; there are many companies in the industry, and most do it virtually identically; reference materials in public libraries and financial databases are plentiful; and there is very little that is new or highly unusual to upset the balance of what is known already—or potentially out there to add to what you need to know. You, the part-time investor who has another career to pursue 40 or more hours a week, can handle the facts and understand what you must in order to become successful in this arena. You *can* do this!

Novelty and hype are absent. One of the major sources of problems for investors in many other industries is that those others are in many cases new and exciting. As a result, they tend to be surrounded by hype. Whether it be a possible cure for a dreaded disease, a newly discovered mineral which will allegedly solve a major industrial problem, or a nifty new product or marketing approach that might change the way consumers spend their money, novelty—the exciting and untested, which cannot yet be proven to be impossible or foolish—attracts investors and therefore attracts investment hype and scam artists. In novel areas, new issues can be sold on hope and loose promises because the concept is so new and the potential so exciting that the investor cannot resist. Such new investment ideas are sold at what hindsight usually proves were ridiculously high prices. Greed of promoters, who artfully manipulate human nature and the desire to take a chance and win, is the overriding element of most exciting new investment ideas. Utilities, by wonderful and comforting contrast are, well, frankly boring. And that is good: the promoters and the hype are absent. Can you imagine a high-pressure securities peddler calling and touting the exciting opportunities available only to you for a limited time if you get in on the ground floor when the electric company puts in a new 20-mile stretch of transmission cable to the next county? Of course not. It's too mundane, too fundamentally measurable and understandable, and cannot conceivably excite you to believe in unreasonably high financial reward. So the promoters are absent and the incidence of overvalued securities propped up by a fad is low. There is basically only one major danger of hype in utilities: beware the sales professional selling you high yield. This danger is very alluring, so we devote Chapters 11 and 12 to exposing it.

Emotional content is low or at least controllable. With very few exceptions, investing in the utilities industry is by definition an experience lacking in highly emotional content. This is good in the investment field, where all too often the investor gets excited (and buys or holds) when news is very positive (defining a high point in the market) and then later panics (and sells or fails to buy) when the news is temporarily bad (defining a low area in the market). Natural or human-made disasters are basically the only unavoidable elements in investing in utilities. Even these elements are somewhat manageable, however. For example, one can decide not to take any nuclear power risk by steering clear of electric utilities with such exposure in their fuel mixes (see Chapter 21 for lists). One can seek to reduce exposure to the hazards of gas explosion by steering clear of earthquake-prone areas of the country; one can identify the states most frequently ravaged by hurricanes and choose to invest elsewhere. While a weather disaster can strike anywhere, one can lessen the odds by diversifying and/or by careful selection of locations. Or one can look at history and realize that whatever the natural disaster may be, there is insurance carried by the industry and there is always rebuilding and a new start: the stock price may be hurt temporarily but the utility survives.

A human-made disaster such as a mistake in running a nuclear power plant is an undeniable but remote possibility. The consequences are incalculable, but we know without requiring the exact details they would be financially devastating. We came close to a meltdown at Three Mile Island in 1979. The individual investor can decide whether to avoid the low-probability but high-stakes risk of such investments altogether. Essentially, TMI changed the regulatory climate permanently, and electric utilities by the dozens have cut or omitted dividends (and, in a handful of cases, have gone into bankruptcy) as a result.

These are operational/financial/regulatory risks carrying major emotional impact that must be understood. We develop these ideas in a later chapter. But with these very few and well-defined exceptions, utility investing is by nature an unexciting pursuit. And that fact itself helps the investor by steering him or her away from the emotional rollercoaster inherent in many other industries. Utility stock prices are a relatively safe haven in the emotional storm of Wall Street's frequent mood swings from too low to too high.

Information is easily available. There is a good deal of information on the utilities industry quite readily available to the nonprofessional investor. Tracking supply, demand, growth, and rate decisions is not impossible. Virtually every brokerage firm that has a credible research department follows utility stocks. There are reports readily available for you to study. *The Value Line Investment Survey* covers many dozen utilities and you can study and compare their reports readily. Newspapers, chart services, and S&P individual stock reports provide the key data on dividends and earnings trends in easily accessible form, as do popular financial databases. What makes investing in utilities manageable and successfully doable for the individual investor is precisely the large supply of information which is readily comparable.

As will be developed in depth in Parts II and III of this book, there is really just one critical fundamental variable to track: the growth rate of the dividend stream. You can follow this data to the exclusion of all others if you wish, and if you follow a common-sense approach to deal with the key information the board of directors supplies via their dividend decisions, you will be successful as a utilities investor. This book provides that system and explains why it will work for you. All you need is the discipline to follow the system.

There is one danger, however, and I think of it as the danger of the rearview mirror: as investors, we develop comfort zones from owning investments that have been successful for us. We get warm and fuzzy feelings about stocks that have treated us well. We must guard against complacency and take action when our signals say the time to sell has come. This will be essential to your success in investing in utilities. While this is a conservative and long-term oriented program rather than a speculative or get-rich-quick approach, a stock once bought must not be considered a hold-forever situation. Good selling is as crucial to success as good buying.

You and the industry are a natural match. You, the reader, are the final element in a successful investment program. If you got past the first chapter and decided that your investment objective is indeed financial success rather than emotional thrills, you are well suited to success via utilities investing. You have reached a stage in life when you know it is time to get serious about your financial future, to stop "playing" in the market and start working at a sensible and solid plan. You are emotionally tuned to the pace and to the risk/reward mix. You will be comfortable with the relative lack of high pressure and tension, the relative simplicity of the decision process that will be revealed in following chapters, and the moderate-risk environment. You are tuned in to making reasonable money over the long term and have decided, either due to emotional makeup or as the result of painful past experience, that you do not need to reach for the big gain at the risk of taking the big loss. You and the utilities industry are well matched, and this match will contribute to your success. All you need to do is know the rules and have the self-discipline to follow them. That is what the following sections of the book are about.

PART TWO

UNDERSTANDING THE BIG PICTURE

Risks: Defining and Understanding Them

Make no mistake: there is risk inherent in every type of investment. Hold money under the mattress and the risks are theft, loss of purchasing power to inflation, and the lost rewards of other possibilities foregone. Put money in a federally insured high-yield bank CD, and the risks include delays in payout of FDIC insurance in the event of failure; possible loss of purchasing power after taxes; and the chance that investing in a bond or a utility stock would have produced a greater return total, including capital appreciation, in the same period. Buy a government bond and the risks (even if remote) include political revolution, renunciation of public debts, and price decline if interest rates rise. Buy a short-term T-Bill, and the major risk remains opportunity loss.

Investing in utility stocks is not a panacea, although the results can be very rewarding to those who follow the risk-reducing principles developed in this book. There definitely are some risks. It is well to list and discuss them at the outset. As actuaries would note, there is both a severity and a likelihood associated with each kind of risk. Stand in the rain during an electrical storm and there are two dangers: being hit by lightning is a very small possibility with potentially fatal consequences. Being soaked to the bone and catching a cold is highly likely but has only a minor cost—unless you are to debut at the Metropolitan Opera the following week! So, for each risk of investing in utility stocks one must note both the likelihood and the implied severity of the potential problem. While the likelihood and severity of a particular event-caused loss cannot be measured precisely in investing, fortunately there are very often visible warning signs when the risk of adverse results is rising. The investor may ignore the warnings only at his or her peril.

RISK #1: DIVIDEND REDUCTION

The greatest risk is the chance that the dividend stream will be reduced. This will impair not only the investor's income stream but also his or her capital. The latter effect is due to the market's capitalizing the newly declared dividend rate instead of the older, higher one. Investors perceive a dividend cut as a sudden event. In the sense that the board of directors meets on a certain day, changes the dividend rate, and issues a press release, that is true. But a dividend reduction by a utility company is virtually never a surprise to the investor who has been watching the signs. A pattern of change often precedes the dividend cut. High payout ratios, adverse regulatory decisions, and deceleration of the growth rate of dividends, especially to zero growth, are among the critical danger signals. (For further discussion, see Chapters 14 and 15.)

RISK #2: RISING INTEREST RATES

The second greatest risk to the utility investor is an adverse movement in interest rates. Depending upon the degree of change in rates, this can be a major danger. For example, if long-term rates should double, a constant dividend stream would be capitalized at twice the former rate, resulting in a 50% reduction in stock price. A $20 utility share paying a $1.00 annual dividend (thus yielding 5%) would decline to $10 per share if interest rates doubled and forced a 10% yield from the same dividend payment. While the risk of an interest-rate rise is not to be dismissed (particularly after a long decline such as occurred from 1981 through 1993), there are ways to guard against this risk. One is to be vigilant and realistic about the news background. If inflation shows signs of increasing, inevitably interest rates will not be far behind. If the Federal Reserve raises the discount rate, it is a major signal of policy: tighter money. One can never know in advance the future course of interest rates. But one can be resolute in refusing to ignore the trend. If rates have changed by one or two points, the tide has definitely turned and should not be ignored. Large changes in interest rates do not take place overnight (even the shock of a war or an OPEC price increase takes some time to be fully played out in interest rates).

While the seriousness of an increase in rates cannot be dismissed, the effect on the utility investor will be reduced if he or she is holding stocks whose dividends are rising rather than standing still. Referring again to the stock paying a $1.00 annual dividend: if the dividend grows by 5% per year compounded, in 10 years the rate will be $1.628 per share. If interest rates doubled during that 10 years, even the investor who refused to note the rise in rates and sell would suffer only an 18.6% loss of capital (stock would decline from $20 to $16.28 per share) rather than a 50% decline. In this sense (but not in the sense of a guarantee of annual cash income) one might think of a utility stock as a perpetual bond: it would be better to hold a bond whose income is higher each year than one whose coupons are fixed, if interest rates are to rise. So, in summary, the risk of rising interest rates can be mitigated in two ways: do not ignore the economic macro trends, and hold only stocks whose dividends are being increased at a fairly constant percentage rate each year.

RISK #3: STOCK-SPECIFIC DISCOUNT-RATE INCREASES

A more subtle risk for the utilities investor, but nevertheless a real and not insignificant one, is that the stock chosen will suffer a relative loss of favor. For example, in an otherwise stable interest-rate climate, a particular stock could gradually move from a position where its yield is average to one where the market requires an above-average cash yield. Suppose a particular utility stock paying a $2.00 annual dividend is bought at about $33.375 at a time when the market demands a cash yield of 6% for that company's stock. If investor perceptions of the company collectively change to the degree that later a 7% cash yield is required, the shares will have declined to about $28.625, causing over a 14% paper (but real) loss of capital. If the overall level of interest rates were unchanged while this happened to a specific utility stock, it would be evidence of increased concern on the part of investors. If something is perceived as less attractive or more risky, people simply will pay less for it (or will not buy at all).

The individual investor is, ironically, highly prone to loss in what appears to be a safe investment, such as a utility stock. What seems to be comforting evidence that all is well is close at hand: the company is still paying that familiar $2.00 per share. Or sometimes, the dividend has even recently been increased slightly. But if the rate of dividend increase has slowed (or if the payout ratio has risen, implying less room for future increases), this is a danger signal. Small and gradual stockmarket losses, much like the creeping effects of old age, cause less alarm than a sudden sharp pain (a dividend cut). If there seems evidence that nothing is seriously wrong (the dividend is intact), the tendency is to let the situation ride in hope of improvement. Ego in the investor makes it difficult to accept losses and mistakes, so the problems and the losses tend to become gradually larger as the stock is held longer. The antidote for this third type of risk is clear: one must follow the signals and be ready to switch to more attractive situations.

Causes of rising relative discount rates for individual utility stocks are of three major varieties: financial, fundamental, and psychological. A financial cause would be a slowdown or halt to the growth rate of dividends, or a rising payout ratio. A fundamental cause would include such things as an adverse change in the political or regulatory climate for the utility (increased concern over acid rain, or inflation sensitivity among rate payers who claim a "right" to a basic convenience such as local telephone service). Psychological effects are seen on occasion even in the relatively unemotional realm of income investing. A couple of severe earthquakes will change investor perceptions of the attraction of natural gas stocks relative to telephone issues, for example. Three Mile Island continues to cast a shadow over electric utility issues with nuclear interests, although the yield differentials have narrowed over the intervening fourteen years.

Whatever the actual cause(s) of the change in collective investor perception of attraction or risk, the evidence can be seen graphically. One merely needs to track the cash yield of the utility stock under study against an average yield of a representative group of peers. While one might use a hand-selected peer group (such as all New England utilities for Boston Edison), there is danger of masking common trends by this approach (e.g., *all* northeastern utilities could be affected by the same adverse trend in oil prices) and thus failing to see an important relative move in yield. A better approach is to use the yield of a broad utility average such as those of Standard & Poor's or Moody's. The accompanying graph shows the drift in relative yield over 10 years for several companies, some of whose fortunes were improving (declining relative yield) and some of whose fortunes were deteriorating. From 1982 through 1989, Detroit Edison was one of the higher-yield electrics, with a flat dividend at $1.68 per year and a high payout ratio. Regulatory compromise was achieved, and in 1990 the dividend was raised. Investors perceived the positive change coming as early as 1989, as reflected in the declining relative yield. Southern Company was a "growth utility" until 1987 when directors failed to raise the $2.14 annual dividend. A hint of improvement came in 1991 when the relative yield declined to 90%; the dividend was finally increased anew in 1992. Nevada Power, by contrast, has seen its dividend stall at $1.60 in the early 1990s and appeared in some danger as early as the end of 1991, based on its rising relative yield.

The single most visible sign of changing attraction in a utility is the information the board of directors conveys through its dividend-growth policy. One need not know or understand, or even agree with, the reason(s); when the growth rate in dividends is changed there is always a reason. A decreased growth rate means trouble ahead. The market takes note of the change in signal, and the price of the stock adjusts. While individual investors are often lured into the quicksand of high yield, sophisticated utility investors seek total return. Total return consists of the current cash return plus the growth rate in dividends over time. When the growth rate is reduced relative to prior history, stock price will be depressed to reflect investors' revised perceptions of risk and reward. The reasons for the change will not always be immediately obvious, and only sometimes will be stated. The absence or invisibility of stated reasons for the change is irrelevant: the directors have spoken by their actions. The inescapable conclusion is that a change in dividend-growth rate cannot be ignored, for it is an official signal from those in the best position to know that the company's risk environment has changed. So the way for the utilities investor to control the discount-rate risk is to take action without delay whenever a modified dividend policy signals a change in outlook.

SUMMARY

In summary, there are three sources of danger for the utilities investor: dividend risk, interest-rate risk, and valuation risk. The antidote in each case is closely monitoring signals that are clear and easy to track. These are, respectively: directors' actions, FRB policy shifts, and changing relative yields. But merely observing a sign is not enough; the investor must be prepared to take action (sell!) without any undue loyalty to his or her past holdings. This often troubling area is covered in Chapter 17.

Returns: Thirty Years of Historic Data

No investment plan based upon investing in a single medium should be considered complete since by its nature such a plan is not diversified. This principle applies to the utilities industry just as it would to investing only in railroads, drug stocks, gold, or real estate. But while no single medium represents a well-rounded investment program, it is nevertheless important to know just how well the particular style of investing in question has performed in the past, both relative to other commonly accepted yardsticks and in absolute terms. This chapter provides the reader with documented history of how investments in utility stocks have performed in the past. The results may prove surprising.

Most investors, if asked to associate a psychic state with utility stocks, would probably chose the word "boring." Chapter 1 dealt with sorting out one's investment priorities and established that profits, not thrills, are the bottom-line goal for people investing seriously with their future financial health and welfare in mind. So being boring is not in itself bad for an investment. What *would* be unfortunate would be to be an underperformer. And, as the data presented in this chapter show, utility stocks have provided very adequate returns over the past several decades in both absolute and relative terms.

For measurement purposes, returns on the Standard & Poor's 385 Industrial Stocks will be compared in this chapter with returns on the Standard & Poor's 45 Utility Companies. These indices were chosen because they are both broader than the comparable Dow-Jones Industrial and Utility Averages, which include 30 and 15 stocks, respectively. In addition, the computation method of the S&P averages is preferable in terms of consistency over time. The Dow-Jones averages are simple arithmetic sums of the prices of the component stocks, divided by a divisor which shrinks over time to adjust for stock splits. In effect, a high-priced stock such as Chevron at $80 has more influence on the direction of the average than does a McDonald's at $50. If Chevron splits two-for-one, then its relative influence is halved. This approach is rather impure from the viewpoint of reflecting what is happening to investors' dollars.

The Standard & Poor's averages are capitalization weighted. This means that each of the stocks in the average is weighted by the number of shares outstanding times its price. Thus the change in the average is weighted more by stocks with higher total market value than by others with smaller total value. The effect is to make the S&P average reflect what happens to the total wealth of shareholders who hold those stocks. This is a much purer way of characterizing market action through the use of an "average" of selected stocks. There is no denying that any average containing fewer than all stocks will at times fail to capture all the market's nuances. For example, the S&P and DJIA tend to miss movements in low-priced shares and tend to under-report relative changes in small-capitalization issues—two groups that periodically make significant moves. Even with such limitations, however, the S&P does represent a broad cross section of the market. And it certainly represents the experience of a conservative investor more closely than would the Wilshire 5000. Therefore, the S&P average approach seems the best and most appropriate benchmark for comparison to the results of investing in utilities—a group admittedly conservative, even "boring."

METHOD OF COMPUTING RETURNS

Returns for the table in Appendix IV are measured on a calendar-year basis. The formula is:

$$\frac{\text{(Ending Index Value} + \text{Dividends During Year)}}{\text{Starting Index Value}}$$

Admittedly, this measure of total return fails to account for possible reinvestment of dividends during the year when received. But such a fine computation, if applied to an average, would itself be misleading. This is because each stock pays dividends on its own individual cycle, rather than on the final day of a calendar quarter. Such a detailed computation would be immensely complex and would probably result in little difference in final result. If anything, more frequent reinvestment of dividends is likely to result in a slightly higher average return, for two reasons: dollar cost averaging over more points tends to produce an increased return by lowering the average price paid; and earlier reinvestment of dividends (as contrasted to once annually, at year-end) produces a better result during a period of overall rising prices, since on average earlier will have been better.

Table 7.1 Annual Returns of Utility and Industrial Averages 1960-1991

| | S & P 45 Utilities | | | | S & P 385 Industrials | | | |
Year	Pct. Incr. Divds.	Pct. Cash Yield	Pct. Total Retn	End Val. of 1,000	Pct. Incr. Divds.	Pct. Cash Yield	Pct. Total Retn	End Val. of 1,000
				$24,479				22,898
Best Year	8.0	10.80	45.8		16.7	5.58	36.9	
Worst Year	1.8	3.16	-21.1		-1.9	2.64	-26.5	
Mean	5.0	6.59	11.7		6.2	3.72	11.5	
Std. Dev.	1.9	2.43	15.9		4.5	0.82	15.7	
# Losses (of 32 years)		9				9		
Times down twice in row		2				1		

We apply the annual-return method described above to both the 45 S&P Utility Stocks and the 385 Industrial Stocks, for consistency of approach. To span three decades which included all kinds of financial, political, social, and industrial climates, the study period was started at December 31, 1959. Thus, the first full year for which returns were computed was 1960. The more than thirty years since then have seen a move from low inflation and interest rates, to high inflation and the highest rates since the Civil War, and a return move to reasonably low inflation and interest rates. Thus, there is no bias in selection of time periods examined. The study includes all kinds of economies short of a full-scale repeat of the 1930s' Great Depression.

As illustrated in Appendix IV, the returns on the S&P Utility Average slightly outran those on the S&P Industrials: the average annual rate computed as explained above was 11.67% for utilities and 11.46% for industrials. In the 32 years through 1992, each of the averages had negative total returns in nine years. Utilities were down on a total-return basis two years running twice, and the industrials once. The best and worst years for utilities were more favorable than those for industrials: the utilities' best total return for one year was 45.8% in 1989, while the industrials' best was 36.9% in 1975. The worst year for both averages was 1974, when the utilities lost 21.1% and the industrials 26.5%. That year the OPEC embargo caused both inflation and recession.

The components of total return were somewhat different, however. As might be expected, utilities as reflected in the S&P averages provided a greater average cash dividend yield: 6.6% vs. 3.7%. To achieve a nearly equal annual average total return, the industrial average gained more in price level. Dividends in the S&P industrials fell only twice in the thirty years (in 1970 and 1971). But utilities' dividends on average never fell from year to year. Their growth rate averaged 5.05% and ranged from 1.8% to a high of 8% in individual years.

THE LAST 10 YEARS: A COMFORTING SURPRISE

The period from the market's bottom in August of 1982 to the highs reached in early 1992 has been virtually without precedent in U.S. financial history. Measured by the S&P Industrials, the market rose 2.59-fold from the end of 1981 to the end of 1991. Reinvesting dividends annually as described above, $1,000 invested in "the stock market" as represented by the 385 S&P Industrial Stocks would have grown to $4,991 in 10 years.

What will greatly surprise most individual and professional investors is that a comparable investment in the S&P utilities did even better! The average itself grew 1.93-fold. With dividends "reinvested" annually in the identical manner as above, the $1,000 hypothetical investment would have become $5,807 in the S&P Utilities average. The higher dividend yield on the utility stocks made the difference.

Consistency is an important aspect of investment performance for investors. In the 32 years from 1960-1992, the utilities outperformed the industrials on a total-return basis 18 times. Recent history is both better and quite surprising considering the above-average return on industrial stocks since 1981. Starting with 1981, the utilities' total-return performance was better than that of the industrials in nine of the twelve years through 1992! This was impressive since it occurred during a period when industrial stocks were bid up to historically high earnings multiples on the *hope* of rising future earnings—a hope not yet realized as of this writing.

One cyclical pattern seemed evident, as related to the presidential election cycle. Industrial stocks seem to do worse than utilities in the even-numbered off-election years, but utilities fare worse in the third years of presidential terms: the latter held true in every four-year cycle from 1960 through 1992 except for the year 1975. Perhaps this is related to the reputed tendency to stimulate the economy in the second half of a term, which would tend to raise interest rates and industrial activity in third years. That would hurt utility shares and tend to help industrial stock prices unless the inflation-induced interest-rate increase were severe.

EVEN BETTER THAN AVERAGE

The data discussed above show that utilities slightly more than hold their own in a head-to-head comparison with industrial stocks over long periods. These data relate to *average* performance for utility shares, since the S&P index is by its nature an unmanaged collection of 45 utility stocks.

The main point of studying methods of investment is to discover approaches that are likely to outperform the averages. The alternative to doing good analysis is to save the reading time, sharpen the darts, and sit back and hope blindly for no worse than average luck. The S&P utility average has included various issues for some or all of the past three decades which have experienced significant periods of underperformance. The following are some of the more notable names that have dragged down the utility average for one or several years:

> Cleveland Electric (now Centerior Energy)
>
> Columbia Gas System
>
> Commonwealth Edison
>
> Consolidated Edison of N.Y.
>
> Pacific Gas & Electric
>
> Panhandle Eastern
>
> Philadelphia Electric
>
> Texas Eastern Transmission

The objective of the utilities-investing system explained in this book is to weed out companies that are headed for underperformance and to keep invested funds working in companies likely to continue to provide above-average returns. How this is done systematically will be explained in detail in Chapters 13 through 16. The result of such positive selection is performance above the norm, which this chapter has shown to be mildly above the mean result for investing in industrial stocks. The key difference, as was discussed in Chapter 2, is achieved by avoiding losses. For the utilities investor, loss avoidance is both financially rewarding and psychologically comforting.

An investment program, remember, must give the owner enough comfort so that he or she is not scared into selling out at or near the occasional bottoms. This applies to both the overall portfolio and individual issues. To whatever degree stock selection—and de-selection!—can help the investor sidestep the trap of panic selling, it can make a major contribution to a positive overall result.

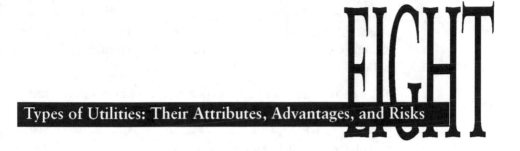

Types of Utilities: Their Attributes, Advantages, and Risks

There are four major categories of utility stocks, not including hybrid or combination types of companies. Most numerous are electric companies. Second most numerous are gas utilities, which can be broken down for analysis purposes into (long-distance) transmission versus (local) distribution types. Telephone utilities are a third major type, and again there is a distinction (which came into being with the 1984 AT&T court case) between long-distance versus local companies. Finally there are the relatively few publicly traded water companies. The most common combination or hybrid type of utility company is one that operates both electric and gas services. Also, a relative handful are even more diverse in that they are holding companies with an assortment of electric, gas, and telephone companies—and occasionally even a water company—in their portfolios. This chapter discusses the important features of each group and places some emphasis on identifying the important risk elements which investors should be aware of.

COMMON ATTRIBUTES

All types of utilities share certain features, although some of the attributes are more extreme or more critical in one type than in another. All are quite capital intensive. This means that there is a large minimum monetary investment required to be in the business—large in terms of hundreds of millions or even several billions of dollars, and large relative to the revenue stream generated by the business. All utilities are regulated by state and/or federal bodies, which set standards and regulate pricing and thereby the potential returns that the companies can achieve. And, very significantly in terms of potential impact on investors, utilities provide services considered "essential" basic needs in advanced civilized economies; their pricing and their profits are therefore subject to populist and often economically ignorant political forces.

The fact that most utilities operate as monopolies under official-grant by the public authorities adds to the scrutiny, the justification for regulation, and the heat of the debate. As discussed in Chapter 6, the relative lack of economic sophistication by the public, the press, and even in some cases the public-sector regulators are very real and potentially dangerous factors which affect investors' returns. While U.S. society is economically organized at least nominally on capitalist principles, the same kind of philosophy that asserts that health care is a "basic human right" has little regard for the rights of investors to have their capital safeguarded against seizure: electric power and phone service (not to mention water) are regarded by some as such basic needs that they choose to ignore the reality that these are economic goods that cannot be provided either free or at a loss. Public pressure, often stirred up by media that run stories about the poor versus the giant corporation, is a source of danger to the investor, especially in jurisdictions where public utility commissions are popularly elected rather than appointed.

The balance of this chapter explores key elements of each of the four utility subsectors. The matrix in Appendix III summarizes major attributes, advantages, and risks, as a brief overview for the investor concerned with overall themes and comparisons.

ELECTRIC UTILITIES

Electric power providers are given an exclusive franchise, by the relevant state or local governments, to operate within a given geographical area. In return, they subject themselves to rate setting and to regulation of allowable rates of return, and they are required to provide service on the basis of a nondiscriminatory rate structure to any customer no matter how remotely located. Electric utilities are highly capital intensive. In addition, with the exception of marginal sources such as small dams and cogeneration by industrial plants, the minimum unit of added plant investment is very large. This poses a not-inconsiderable risk to the electric utility stock investor: a decision to add generating capacity had better be correct and correctly timed or the invested capital may be disallowed by the regulators, forcing write-offs and probable dividend reduction or omission. Commonwealth Edison in 1992 was a good example. Nuclear power plants, which take longest to bring on line (about 12 years) and which involve the largest minimum unit of investment, pose the greatest investment risks. Ask the former shareholders of Public Service of New Hampshire.

Electric utilities are also subject to significant, ever-changing environmental regulation, which comes at large financial cost. Nuclear energy entails the need for fail-safe planning and execution. No new nuclear facilities have been proposed since the mid-1980s, reflecting both a slowdown in power-usage growth rates and a recognition by managements that the risks are so large as to potentially bankrupt a company undertaking such construction. Burning oil contributes to air pollution and adds to the demand for imported oil, involving a company in geo-political risk and raising the balance of payments deficit. In the 1970s many oil-burning electric utilities suffered badly from a period of regulatory lag, during which they were not allowed to pass through fast-rising raw material (fuel) costs. Now, despite economically ignorant public opposition, fuel adjustment clauses have been adopted that allow reasonable automatic rate changes (in both directions) with little or no delay.

Coal, once the principal source of electric power generation in the United States, brings its own environmental problems, including sulfur dioxide emissions contributing to acid rain. Burning releases heat which is alleged to contribute to global warming and possible destruction of the ozone layer. It is unclear what the total future financial burden of burning coal cleanly will be; ultimately it *should* be borne by the power consumer but there is risk of delay and politically motivated misallocation to the stockholder. The law and the regulations and the regulators keep changing, but the primary direction is clearly toward increased regulation.

Risk of nuclear accident remains a cloud over electric utility companies operating, or partially owning, such generation facilities. The Three Mile Island accident in 1979 focused concern on such risk even though, fortunately for everyone, a total meltdown was narrowly avoided. The Price-Anderson Act has mandated a system of mutual insurance under which every U.S. utility using nuclear generation has a financial obligation in the event of a nuclear accident at any such plant. The maximum financial impact per company is a not-trivial sum: $560 million!

While the differential has narrowed, nuclear electric companies continue to sell at higher yields than their non-nuclear counterparts. This reflects added risk as well as the fact that some investors simply choose not to invest in nuclear power just as some others boycott tobacco or alcohol when investing. Chapter 21, which treats the nuclear power issue in more detail, includes a table listing electric companies that have no present nuclear generation and none scheduled to come on line in the future.

A new potential liability area has arisen for electric utilities in the early 1990s. Some scientific studies have begun to link the electromagnetic fields generated by high-voltage overhead transmission cables to elevated incidence of cancer among nearby residents. Some years may pass before eventual disposition of the issue, but investors should monitor legal trends rather than be surprised.

Managements of electric utilities in the 1980s in many cases embarked upon a diversification strategy (investor Warren Buffett refers to this often-risky course as di-WORSE-ification!). They bought oil and gas and coal reserves in many cases. In other instances they went far afield into such competitive or cyclical ventures as cable TV, banks and S&Ls, real estate, and others.

Generally, the result has been predictable: managements and boards accustomed to the relatively well defined confines of a highly regulated basic business found unexpected and often huge problems in unfamiliar (to them) territory; shareholders lost a lot of money. The late 1980s and the early 1990s have seen an unwinding of such ties, accompanied by write-offs and in some cases dividend reductions or omissions. Relatively few companies have diversified without pain, and it remains to be seen if those few have yet to realize such costs in the future or if they have truly invested successfully.

One positive trend among electric utilities has been the tendency toward consolidation via merger. There are natural economies of scale to be achieved by such combinations, particularly within a single regulatory jurisdiction. For example, if all the utilities in Kansas were one, they would need only a single staff to interface with regulators; they would need only one shareholder relations department and one dividend-reinvestment plan staff; they would need only one economic forecasting and budgeting function, one president, and one board of directors.

Savings from consolidation can be shared by shareholders and the public, creating a potential win/win equation. Typically, the company acquired will gain a small benefit for its shareholders in terms of values of shares exchanged. The investor should never expect a large windfall in a utility merger, such as those occasionally received in less regulated industries where strategic alliances and/or deeply discounted stock prices sometimes generate major merger premiums for the acquired companies. There is sometimes a double benefit available to the utility investor who buys small companies' shares: these companies are the most likely merger targets and they also sell at moderately higher yields that reflect a slight market inefficiency caused by minimum position sizes among institutional investors. A caution, however: mergers of regulated companies take several years rather than several months and can be defeated by intervenors and regulators. The case of California's huge SCEcorp and San Diego Gas & Electric in the early 1990s is a classic example.

One of the major positive attributes of natural gas is that it is clean burning. It is therefore often referred to as the fuel of choice for the environmentally conscious future. The most commonly cited negative is the danger of explosion. This risk exists at the individual consumption point (in the home), in general along transmission lines and at storage facilities and most dramatically in areas prone to earthquake. Natural gas utilities are capital intensive, although less highly so than electric utilities.

Transmission companies operate the long-distance pipelines that transport huge volumes of fuel from the producing areas (and international ports) of the nation to the consuming areas such as major industrial and population centers. Examples of this kind of company are Tennessee Gas Transmission (owned by Tenneco), Consolidated Natural Gas, Columbia Gas System, and Transco. The main risk to such companies is in the form of regulation. Since the early 1980s the federal regulatory environment has changed considerably. The major sea change has been a series of decisions requiring "open access." This has meant that pipelines are now required to allow gas users, if the latter wish, to contract directly to buy gas from a producer and separately contract for its transport via an interstate pipeline. The analogy is an auto producer buying steel from a distant mill and separately arranging for its delivery via railroad. In the past, pipelines bundled the transport function and the merchant function (buying and reselling the gas) into a single overall delivered price and were allowed to refuse to unbundle the functions.

The regulatory revolution of the 1980s brought severe financial consequences for many pipeline companies. The reason is that during the old era in which they could impose bundled pricing, many pipelines contracted for delivery of minimum fixed quantities of gas from producers at what later proved to be unsustainably high prices. Such contracts were made following the energy shortages of the 1970s. Pipelines were afraid to be short of supply and were trying to avoid being forced to buy needed marginal gas on the spot market at unpredictable prices. So they signed up for guaranteed supplies in what became known as take-or-pay arrangements: in exchange for an assurance of supply, the pipeline company obligated itself to accept certain minimum quantities or to pay for them anyway.

Then the rules changed and the pipelines no longer were the only buyers of gas. Unless they were able to renegotiate their contracts and substitute end-users' demand for their own, they faced multi-billion-dollar liabilities. Take-or-pay was the cause of the 1991 Chapter 11 filing by Columbia Gas System. Other systems have taken huge financial charges and are still working out their contracts; dividend cuts and omissions have resulted (see Chapter 10).

Gas distribution companies are local in nature, supplying connections between the pipeline supplier and the final gas users such as homes, factories, and industrial plants or shopping centers. In some cases such companies have been dragged into the take-or-pay problem by being forced by regulators to assume part of the financial burdens of their upstream suppliers. Such sharing of costs has added to the price of gas; users have a choice of fuels, so suppliers have not been able to pass along all such costs. Thus, the shareholder has borne some of the burden.

Local gas distribution companies also provide the investor with more direct exposure to local economic conditions, for better or for worse. The smaller the geographic territory, the greater the possible risk this represents. Rhode Island's Providence Energy, formerly Providence Gas, is an example of such concentrated exposure as compared, for example, with the much larger Peoples [sic] Corp., which serves Chicago and other parts of Illinois.

Local distribution companies face the potential positive or negative effects of fuel substitution by residential and business users. If their service territories are fairly large and no customer accounts for a major share of their business, the effects can be only minimal. Contrast this, in terms of scale of impact, with the effect on a pipeline if a major distribution company should switch its gas source from a Canadian producer to a U.S. Gulf Coast source, or vice versa: a different pipeline gets the business.

Gas utility stocks generally sell at lower yields than electric companies situated in the same regulatory jurisdictions. Until the 1990s the gas companies displayed much less tendency to cut or eliminate dividends. This has changed in recent years. When the take-or-pay obligations are finally sorted out, this differential will again be justified, since the electric companies are more capital intensive and involve greater minimum capital-project costs when expanding. The electric companies produce energy, while the pipelines (to the extent they separate the functions) buy and transport gas and do not necessarily assume the risks of energy exploration and development.

Just as some electric utilities added risk via diversification, a number of pipeline companies added to their risk (of course, not realizing it fully at the time) by vertically integrating into energy production. They did this in an effort to assure supply and to insulate themselves (in the period before regulation altered the rules) from changing energy prices or to gain the benefit of expected rises in prices. Unfortunately, the companies did not act as contrarians: too many bought energy reserves or entire energy production companies during the period of high raw energy prices in the late 1970s and early 1980s. Local distribution companies, typically smaller in size and financial resources and subject to intense local regulation and scrutiny, have been much less aggressive in acquiring their own energy sources.

TELEPHONE UTILITIES

In the future, the terminology may change: "communications companies" seems more appropriate as the range of available services has broadened. Formerly the "phone company" offered hard-wired telephone service; now it may be involved as well in cellular phone service, paging technology, manufacturing of communications equipment, and cable television. Many telephone companies have diversified into unrelated areas such as real estate, venture capital, and financial services. The utilities investor must decide whether he or she wants all this or prefers plain vanilla. Regulation and technology are both in flux. This change in the environment presents the investor with both potential reward (faster growth via the newer modes) and possible risk (added investment with unknown eventual payback; regulatory change; competition to which management may be culturally unaccustomed; the possibility of significant displacement of past technology by future developments).

Until 1984 there was basically one distinction: there were a few scattered local-service companies such as Rochester Telephone and Cincinnati Bell, and there were the major companies such as GTE and AT&T, which controlled both local service and long-distance facilities. Judge Greene's landmark decision in the AT&T antitrust case created seven regional "baby Bell" companies providing local connections to the national and international network, while American Telephone became a long-distance carrier. Now the investor has a way of choosing regional exposure (Bell Atlantic versus NYNEX versus Southwestern Bell, for example) and of separating the risks and rewards of local and long-distance business. MCI Communications emerged early as a purely long-distance provider.

AT&T has been backed into that role, although its Bell Telephone Laboratories and computer-manufacturing activities provide diversity. Sprint, formerly known as United Telecommunications, is a company which has transmogrified: it was a local phone company that acquired numerous other local companies; it then acquired part of U.S. Sprint; it later bought out its Sprint partner's share; it is now mostly a long-distance company. What was a high-dividend-growth company facing minimal technology and competitive challenges is now a zero-dividend-growth company with a high dividend-payout ratio and very large capital expansion requirements. This evolution illustrates how an investment once made must be constantly monitored even if the holder's intention is long-term investment. What you originally saw (and bought) will not necessarily remain an unchanged "what you get."

A court decision in September 1992 may again impose major change. Now local phone companies must provide open access to their facilities to all comers. This effectively undoes the monopoly local franchise previously common to most areas of the country. Only time will reveal how significant this regulatory/legal shift will be in economic terms. One can only say at this writing that uncertainty has been increased.

Telephone stocks have traditionally sold at lower yields than either gas or electric utility shares. Some differential in this direction appears still justified, but the risks of shifts in regulation as well as the potential for technological displacement may argue for a narrowing. A positive, however, is that it seems likely that demand for communications services will continue to grow faster than that for gas or electric service. A generation ago the nation had perhaps 95% of its homes equipped with phone service. Now many homes have multiple lines (teenagers, independent businesses) and many homes and millions of businesses have added separate lines for fax machines and computer modems. Add car phones and mobile cellular units and there has been an explosion of demand. Our society will become more dependent on everywhere-available communication, and its price continues to slide. As in electronics, lower price creates more demand and new uses. One should therefore expect today's "telephone" utilities to grow faster than the electric or gas companies, although the competitive worlds of the former will be less simple than in times past.

WATER UTILITIES

Scant attention will be given in this volume to the water companies. Except for small local companies traded in local OTC markets, there are but a handful. American Water Works, Etown, Philadelphia Suburban, and United Water Resources are the major names. Traditionally, because rising water rates have led to good earnings and dividend growth, water companies' shares have provided lower yields than electrics. In recent years, however, water stocks' relative yields have drifted upward. Environmental concerns have become more widely understood in the past decade or so. As a society we have become more aware of more sources of health risk than we perceived in earlier times. Costs of ensuring a safe supply of potable water have risen. Supplies have been constrained by redefinition of what is acceptable. The regulatory milieu is shifting, and the direction is not favorable to a for-profit supplier of such a basic commodity as water. The risks seem more likely to increase than to abate. For the investor, available opportunities are certainly more numerous in other utility sectors and appear at least as attractive on an overall risk/reward basis.

This chapter has supplied an overview of the similarities and differences of issues facing investors as they examine electric, gas, telephone, and water companies. For investors in their common stocks, there is fortunately a single common driver for good investment decisions: as detailed in Chapters 14 and 15, the dividend growth rate for any kind of utility is the most critical variable.

Common Stocks vs. Preferreds vs. Bonds

Not all income-oriented investment instruments are alike. Investors must note the differences and tailor the use of various securities to their particular need, risk-bearing strategy, time of life, and the time of the business cycle.

TUTORIAL

The following paragraphs are for the less experienced investor; sophisticates will miss nothing by jumping ahead to the section titled "Investment Implications," on page 71.

The three major classes of corporate securities are bonds (debt) and preferred and common stock (equity). Preferred stock, which is in the middle in terms of seniority, has certain characteristics of both debt and equity, but technically it is the latter. The acid test comes in the event of a corporate bankruptcy: all debtors are satisfied before any preferred holders.

For those unfamiliar with corporate finance, the difference between **debt** and **equity** is most easily explained by analogy to the investment in a home: what the owner holds is the equity; the mortgage company or bank holds the debt. The debt-holder expects to be paid off no matter what; the property owner enjoys all the benefits if values rise and suffers the first and most severe consequences if there is a loss in value. (As the S&L industry crisis has again proved, debt-holders can become involuntary owners and suffer losses; in such cases the original owners are wiped out. Once again, an "oh-that-would-never-really-happen" did happen. History can repeat. Sometimes worst-case scenarios do occur.)

69

Bonds represent the obligation of the issuing corporation to make a series of semi-annual interest payments of a fixed amount, and to repay the face amount of the debt at a certain future time, called the maturity date. Some bonds are secured by the pledge of specific assets such as real estate, an aircraft, or designated miles of a pipeline. Various classes of bonds may have differing priorities of claims, reflected in terms like "senior," "first mortgage," or "junior subordinated." These have important meaning if the debtor company hits hard times.

Preferred stocks represent an unsecured obligation of the issuing corporation to pay a fixed, stated amount of dividends (almost always, quarterly) before any dividends can be paid to the common shareholders. **Preferred dividends** are not legal obligations, as are interest payments, but the failure to declare preferred dividends can result in the holders of the preferred stock, rather than common share owners, electing the company's board, usually after six quarters in arrears. In most cases, preferred dividends are cumulative, meaning that skipped past dividends must be made up before common holders can receive any cash payments. Unlike bonds, most preferred stocks do not have a scheduled final repayment or maturity date for principal; they are potentially perpetual in life span.

Common stock represents the ownership, for better or worse, of the corporation. Common shareholders may enjoy rising dividends over time if the business prospers. They may see smaller dividends or none at all if results are adverse. Common shareholders stand last in line for payments: behind employees, the taxing authorities, suppliers, creditors such as bondholders, and preferred stockholders. But they get *all the rewards* on the margin, in exchange for taking this higher-risk position.

While all three classes of securities will fluctuate in market value, the greatest variability comes with the common, and the least with the bonds. The latter are more strongly pulled toward their face value because they have the most senior claim on assets and cash flow and because they have an expected maturity date, when the face value is expected to be repaid. A bond price will vary less as its maturity date comes closer. Preferred shares, some of which have no sinking fund and therefore a theoretically infinite maturity horizon, will fluctuate more widely in the direction opposite interest rates.

Common stocks have potentially greater upside price room for any given downward move in interest rates, since bonds and preferred stocks are often callable by the company (albeit usually at some premium over face value). When interest rates fall a great deal (as they did in 1992), issuers will replace old debt and preferred with new, lower-cost securities. This process puts a lid on prices for those two, while the common share price may appreciate without such a barrier. Common stocks also stand to benefit from their exclusive right to a possibly rising payments stream. (So-called participating preferred stocks, once used by SCEcorp among others, are now largely extinct.)

Not all utility corporations issue all three types of securities; preferred stocks are the least often used. But utility companies issue preferred stock more routinely than firms in any other industry. In some cases, utility preferreds and bonds may be issued directly by subsidiary companies rather than in the name of the corporate parent; a close reading of the back of the parent's annual report will reveal the related names of interest. The parent's direct obligations are more secure in most cases than those of a single subsidiary. However, regulators will protect an operating subsidiary against the needs of a holding-company parent in order to protect the public (ratepayers).

INVESTMENT IMPLICATIONS

An income-oriented individual investor is well served to hold some mixture of bonds and common stocks. Preferred shares have an occasional place, but it is limited. Usually, the desirable attributes of the preferred can be captured by owning either the bond (greater security of income stream and principal) or the common (upside potential from declining interest rates and/or improving corporate earning power). The desired mix of bonds and commons is determined by the holder's risk profile, the macro business outlook (risk of depression), the stage of the interest-rate cycle, and by the time to a key personal date such as retirement or education funding.

Preferred stocks contain some potential traps for the unwary. First, while they are clearly senior to the common, they are hardly as safe as the bonds. Income-oriented investors have a tendency to assume that a preferred is highly secure and often will buy it for its yield; tough times can prove that thinking fallacious. Preferred shares have two other attributes making them questionable holdings for many individuals: because they are usually issued in fairly small amounts and are held mainly by institutions and corporations, they trade thinly. So it is difficult to get an efficient price execution when buying and selling.

In addition, many older preferreds qualify for a large dividends-received tax credit when held by corporations (but *not* when held by individuals). Therefore, these instruments tend to be priced on an after-tax yield basis, which means their yield in the market is lower than would be justified without the tax advantage. The analogy would be an individual's folly in buying a municipal bond within a tax-free account such as an IRA. The main attraction of utility preferred stocks occurs when the company has been in deep trouble (but stays out of Chapter 11) and is about to stage a recovery. Then, dividend arrears if any will be paid and the preferreds' prices will recover strongly. Prominent examples were Long Island Lighting in 1989 and Pacific Enterprises in 1992.

RELATIVE ADVANTAGES OF BONDS AND OF COMMON STOCKS

One major advantage of holding bonds is the investor's power to layer or "ladder" maturities within the portfolio. This provides a measure of buffering against the uncertainty of the direction of interest rates. Shorter-term bonds will provide the greatest price protection, while long bonds, preferreds, and commons will move a large amount in the direction opposite to interest rates.

The greatest advantage of common stocks—and in the context of this book, utility commons specifically—is the potential for growth of the income stream (which in turn will drive a rise in share price) over time. A central tenet of this book's thesis is that one should exercise strong discipline to focus utility-stock investing on those companies with ongoing growth in dividends and should shun those with stagnant or decelerating payout streams. In fact, a logical corollary is that one should own a utility bond for its high yield and a utility common for its likely total return, but should never assume the risk of holding a high-yield, zero-growth utility common stock. Rather than own a utility common for its high yield, one should accept a high but non-growing yield only when accompanied by the much greater safety that comes with a bond.

Occasionally, some anomalies develop among the yields of utilities' various securities. These should act as signals to the investor. The conditions being revealed by the market may be specific to the company under study, or may be generic to the entire investment landscape at certain rare times. In either case, the implications are important and can portend major opportunity or major potential loss for the investor. The key is to observe changes in relative yields over time, because these reflect the market's collective expectation of risk and potential reward. Relative yield, as discussed here, refers to yield relationships between two or more companies' comparable securities (e.g., 20-year mortgage bonds) or between different securities of the same issuer (e.g., common versus preferred or bond yields).

In any market climate not ruled by extreme fear or euphoria, bond yields of a given company with healthy prospects should be the lowest; preferred yields (adjusted for their tax advantage) would be a bit higher to reflect their greater risk in the corporate hierarchy; and the expected *total return*—not merely the cash yield—on the common stock, which carries the greatest potential risk exposure—as well as the greatest potential long-term reward—should be the highest. The total return on the common is most simply estimated as its current cash yield, *plus* the rate of expected increase in the common dividend (percent per year). The latter is a proxy for the expected appreciation in share price that would be driven by dividend growth in a constant-interest-rate environment.

Most utility common shares sell at lower cash yields than their preferreds or bonds because of the potential for rising dividends. Theoretically, a common stock's share price would react to a change in the actual or expected rate of change in the dividend stream. Table 9.1 snapshots the yields of selected issues of four major eastern electric utilities. The preferreds' yields have not been adjusted for their tax advantage, but clearly would be higher than the bonds' yields after taxes.

Table 9.1 Yields at 12/31/88					
	Common	5-Year	Common		
	Cash	Div Gro	Total	Bonds	Prefd.
Duke Power	6.40	4.67	11.07	10.10	9.63
Detroit Edison	9.67	0.00	9.67	10.68	10.96
Phila. Electric	11.00	0.00	11.00	10.92	11.08
Con. Edison	6.88	10.16	17.04	10.03	9.49

These numbers would suggest that the market did not believe Con Ed directors would continue raising the dividend by 10% (in fact its growth had tapered off to 7% in the latest year) and that there was a bit of hope developing that Detroit Edison might resume some increases in payments. Otherwise the common yields were out of line. One could make the case that unless there were a realistic basis to envision higher common dividends from Philadelphia Electric, its common's yield should be even higher relative to its preferred and bonds. Unless one foresaw a deterioration for Duke Power, its apparent 11% total return on common would be much more attractive than the 11% at Philadelphia Electric unless one literally saw there an equal chance of price appreciation or price damage due to dividend changes.

As suggested by the above comparisons, in an efficient market the securities of various companies in the same industry should perform over a period of time in accordance with their relative fundamental prospects. When comparing two electric utilities, for example, if there is no difference in fuel mix, fuel availability, regulatory climate, or regional growth expectations, the securities should move in roughly equal degree. The major driving force would be the (equal) remaining variable: the changing level of interest rates.

Viewed in isolation from other companies, the different classes of securities of a single issuer will tend to reflect changing perceptions of risk and potential reward for the respective classes of holders. When a company's prospects are solid and stable, one might expect little or no change in the relative yield of its common versus its bonds, for example. At any starting point in time, the company's common stock current yield will be in some percentage relationship to its long-term bonds' yield, perhaps 7% on the common and 9% on the bonds, for a relative current yield of 77.8%. Assuming efficient and liquid markets, improving or worsening perceptions about the company will drive a change in this percentage relationship.

To illustrate these phenomena, consider the yield behavior of the common stocks and selected bonds and preferreds of several large electric utilities during 1989. By almost any measure, interest rates declined moderately on balance in that calendar year. So not surprisingly, pipeline, telephone, water, and electric utility securities tended to rise. The six electric utilities in our example all saw quite similar declines in their bonds' yields to maturity (to limit possible distortion, the bonds and preferreds examined all had dividend or coupon rates around 9.5%). Using 1988 year-end yield-to-maturity levels for each company as an index of 100, by year-end the six bonds' yields had declined to indexes of between 88 and 92 — quite a tight clustering. In more familiar terms, if the starting bond yield to maturity (YTM) had been 9.50%, a drop to 90 in its indexed yield would be caused by a drop of 0.95% to a new YTM of 8.55% (see Table 9.2).

Table 9.2 Bonds' Yield Comparison			
	Year-end 1988	Year-end 1989	Ending Index
Con.Edison	10.03	9.08	91
Detroit Ed.	10.68	8.91	92
Duke Power	10.10	8.91	88
Pacific G&E	10.33	9.38	91
Phila. Elec.	10.92	9.77	89
SCEcorp.	10.00	9.23	92

Yields of the companies' preferred stocks surveyed (again with roughly 9.5% nominal dividend rates) also moved in a close band, to between 85% and 93% of the year-earlier levels. (The wider range might reflect the slightly greater price variance in preferreds, which trade less actively than bonds; the more heavily traded preferreds were selected to help limit this effect.) The relative similarity of the bonds' and preferreds' moves indicates no change in tax laws and relatively stable expectations about risks to the cash returns of senior holders, as between the two classes (see Table 9.3).

Table 9.3 Preferreds' Yield Comparison				
	Year-end 1988	Year-end 1989	Bonds' Index	Index
Con.Edison	9.49	8.30	87	91
Detroit Ed.	10.96	9.71	89	92
Duke Power	9.63	8.76	91	88
Pacific G&E	10.03	9.10	91	91
Phila. Elec.	11.08	9.45	85	89
SCEcorp.	9.02	8.40	93	92

One might expect that the relative yields on the common shares would move the most, since these are traded in a more emotion-driven market and since the equity holder feels the greatest effect of any news of fundamental changes. In fact, with one exception the six companies' yield indexes moved in a close cluster to between 80 and 87, declining a bit more deeply than those of the senior securities. The latter might indicate rising confidence or perhaps investors' greater perceived need to gain possible rising future income streams. Detroit Edison was the exception, its yield decreasing by 32% during 1989 (see Table 9.4). Apparently the market sensed a really improving situation for common holders.

Table 9.4 Commons' Yield Comparison			
	Year-end 1988	Year-end 1989	Index
Con.Edison	6.88	5.91	86
Detroit Ed.	9.67	6.62	68
Duke Power	6.40	5.56	87
Pacific G&E	8.00	6.36	80
Phila. Elec.	11.00	9.51	86
SCE corp.	7.66	6.44	84

In fact, the market proved correct: in February 1990 directors of Detroit Edison raised the common dividend by nearly 6% to $1.78 per share annually. This was a major positive signal since it was the first dividend increase since 1981. During much of the interim, Detroit Edison suffered regulatory distress with its troubled Fermi 2 nuclear station, had a very high payout ratio, and was periodically suspected as ready to cut the dividend. Its yield was alarmingly high. This was, in fact, a relatively rare case of a high-yield utility whose yield did not become ephemeral via dividend cut or omission.

For purposes of this chapter, the key point is that the market saw the Detroit Edison change coming and the relative yield of its common reflected that perception. Chapter 19 deals with relative yields in more detail since they represent a useful predictive tool.

Worth note here was the fate of Philadelphia Electric's common holders. In April 1990 PE's directors reduced their dividend by 45% from $2.20 to $1.20 per year. Its common shareholders had taken the risk of a high current yield. Since 1984, the last time the dividend had been raised, they had seen the caution flag from directors: no dividend increases. In the first two months of 1989, PE's price had fallen somewhat more than the Dow-Jones Utility Average did: 13% versus 9.3%. An adverse regulatory decision in late February rocked the stock—already yielding 11% —with a one-day 10% decline followed by further erosion. By the day before directors met in April, the stock, at $16.50, was yielding an *apparent* 13.23%. A week later it had fallen to $15.50, where the new dividend rate yielded about 7.74%. That fat 13%+ had literally proved more apparent than real.

The critical question following the dividend cut was what to do. (Actually, as discussed in Chapter 14, a reliable signaling system had flashed a sell signal years earlier!) With a new yield of 7.74%, should common holders of PE have retained their positions? As detailed in Table 9.5, their stock was now yielding in the range of some other big eastern utilities (still signaling some perceived risk) but was providing a yield slightly below that of its own bonds. The bonds and preferred stocks showed slight positive reaction to the cut in common dividends. This was appropriate since smaller common utilities paid out mean more assets left to protect senior holders' interests.

Table 9.5 Yields on Eastern Electric Commons, Late April 1990*	
	Yield
Boston Edison	8.50
Pub Svc E & G	8.45
New Engl Elec	8.12
Phila Electric	**7.74**
Con. Ed of N Y	7.71
Balt Gas & El	7.37

*One week after Philadelphia Electric dividend cut.

Returning to the bedrock rationale for owning utility common stocks, one must either receive a higher current cash yield than on the company's bonds—to compensate for greater risk—or one must expect enough growth in dividends (and certainly expect no risk of a cut) to provide an overall higher total return than from the lower-risk bonds. With Philadelphia Electric's bonds yielding about 9.5% in April 1990 and its common yielding 7.74%, a buyer of the common (and therefore also a holder!) must expect at least a 1.75% per year rise in dividends merely to equalize the yield, let alone to provide any compensation for the greater risk of the commonholder versus the bondholder.

Looking at it from another angle, why should one have accepted a 7.74% cash return from Philadelphia Electric, which had had enough problems to have just reduced its dividend, when one could get 7.71% from Consolidated Edison, which had upped its dividend rate by nearly 7% as recently as January? To be blunt, the case for holding Philadelphia Electric at a price of $15.50 was still far from convincing. Another factor militating for sale was that most taxable holders would now have a paper loss that could be turned into cash via a tax deduction by realizing that loss (the stock had traded above $16 consistently since 1985). Thus the stock was worth more if sold than if held, net of tax effects. At year's end one could logically expect to see tax-selling pressure on the stock for this reason—a further reason for beating the rush to sell.

As illustrated by the Detroit Edison rise in 1989 and the pre-dividend-cut Philadelphia Electric drop in early 1990, the market generally senses upcoming fundamental events and trends. This is especially true in widely followed industry groups, where the market is fairly efficient. This is true of each of the utility groups, although perhaps least so of the small number of water companies. To track the changes in perception, one must follow yields over time, and in particular relative yields. High-yield situations will occasionally work out, but in the large majority of cases they are flashing warnings that should not be ignored.

One footnote to that statement is that in the middle range of the pack there can be bargains due to inefficient markets, particularly among smaller-capitalization issues. Chapters 19 and 20 deal in more detail with market inefficiencies and with relative yields.

SUMMARY

The point of this chapter has been to describe the various reasons for owning common shares as opposed to preferreds or bonds. As illustrated, one class of securities in a single company can move quite differently from the others under certain circumstances. And even though all three provide significant current cash returns, the holder should not let this create a false sense of inviolate security when news from the company becomes bad. Utility common shares hold the greatest potential but also the greatest risks among the three securities classes.

Dividends Are No Longer Sacred

Every investor, and not least those concentrating on utilities, must remember that the economic, political, and business scene is constantly changing. In investing as in business management, one should assume that to plan for *lack* of change is to invite failure! This means that what was once (perhaps at the time of purchase) considered a safe or positive situation will not necessarily remain so. The investor must be on guard to avoid complacency—to avoid sanctifying a long-held belief just because it was once true. One must always take a questioning approach in investing, particularly since a stock position already held tends to collect its own lore and aura in the mind of the holder. One must always watch the market itself for signals that change is perceived as happening or likely. In the area of utilities investing, the market is generally quite efficient. Therefore a meaningful price movement of one stock against the group should be taken as a signal that someone else (or many others) knows something that would be worthwhile to discover and evaluate. The investor must detach the ego while keeping the brain's evaluative processes in full gear.

One of the most important lessons utility investors must learn and internalize is this: *dividends are no longer sacred.* True, in the eyes of the recipient the quarterly dividend is the most central and critical element in the buying and holding decision. And a stream of seemingly dependable past payments creates a sense of comfort and apparent surety. But that perception and feeling of the individual investor must not be projected onto the board of directors. The utility's board certainly does not *want* to disappoint investors or spoil its string of consecutive or rising dividends. But the board deals in multi-million- and sometimes billion-dollar realities. Perhaps in the past there was a strong predisposition to declare the dividend almost no matter what. Now, despite what the investor might wish, that is no longer the case!

Several factors have decreased the safety of the dividend:

• Consolidated Edison in April 1974 shocked Wall Street by omitting its dividend; many other utilities have cut or omitted dividends since that time, so an adverse declaration action is no longer a headline event (see Table 10.1, History of Dividend Reductions and Omissions for some sobering facts).

TABLE 10.1 History of Dividend Reductions and Omissions: 1973-1993

AlaTenn Resources	Gas	Cut, 1987
Arkla	Gas	Cut, 1992
Bangor Hydro-Electric	Elec	Cut, 1984
Berkshire Gas	Gas	Cut, 1991
Boston Edison	Elec	Cut, 1989
Centerior Energy	Elec	Cut, 1987
Central Hudson Gas & Elec	Elec	Cut, 1988
Central Maine Power	Elec	Cut, 1984; Cut, 1985
CMS Energy	Elec	Omitted, 1984
Coastal Corp.	Gas	Cut, 1984
Columbia Gas System	Gas	Cut, 1988; Omitted, 1991
Commonwealth Edison	Elec	Cut, 1992
Consol. Edison Co. of NY	Elec	Omitted, 1974
C-TEC Corp.	Phone	Omitted, 1989
Duquesne Light	Elec	Cut, 1986
Eastern Utilities Assoc	Elec	Cut, 1991
El Paso Electric	Elec	Omitted, 1989
ENSERCH Corp.	Elec	Omitted, 1985
Energy	Gas	Cut, 1986; Cut 1993
General Public Utilities	Elec	Cut, 1979; Omitted, 1980
Green Mountain Power	Elec	Cut, 1974
Gulf States Utilities	Elec	Cut, then Omitted, 1986

Illinois Power	Elec	Omitted, 1989
Kansas City P & L	Elec	Cut, 1986
Kansas Gas & Electric	Elec	Cut, 1986
K N Energy	Gas	Cut, 1987
Long Island Lighting	Elec	Omitted, 1984
Maine Public Service	Elec	Cut, 1984; Omitted, 1985
Midwest Resources	Elec	Cut, 1990; Cut, 1992
Montana Power	Elec	Cut, 1985
NY State Electric & Gas	Elec	Cut, 1988
Niagara Mohawk Power	Elec	Omitted, 1989
NIPSCO	Elec	Omitted, 1986
Ohio Edison	Elec	Cut, 1990
ONEOK, Inc.	Gas	Omitted, 1988
Pacific Enterprises	Gas	Cut, 1991; Omitted, 1992
Pacific Gas & Electric	Elec	Cut, 1988
Pacificorp	Elec	Cut, 1993
Panhandle Eastern	Gas	Cut, 1990
Philadelphia Electric	Elec	Cut, 1990
Pinnacle West Capital	Elec	Cut, then Omitted, 1989
Portland General	Elec	Cut, 1990
Providence Energy	Gas	Cut, 1975; Cut, 1991
PSI Resources	Elec	Cut, 1984; Omitted, 1986
P S of New Mexico	Elec	Cut, then Omitted, 1989
P S of New Hampshire	Elec	Omitted, 1984
Rochester Gas & Electric	Elec	Cut, 1987
Southwest Gas	Gas	Cut, 1991
Tenneco	Gas	Cut, 1991
Transco	Gas	Cut, 1975; Cut, 1987; Cut, 1991
Tucson Electric Power	Elec	Cut, 1989; Omitted, 1990
United Illuminating	Elec	Cut, 1984
Westcoast Energy	Gas	Cut, 1986

Note: Inclusion on this list does not imply that a company is in present danger of further adverse dividend actions. Indeed, some companies listed above restored and further increased dividends subsequent to the cuts and/or omissions listed.

• By the late 1980s most utilities had completed or greatly scaled down their generation construction programs; the necessity for constantly raising new capital, in part from equity, has become much less urgent than in the past. Continuing dividends were supported more firmly when frequent capital raising was necessary.

• Regulation generally has become more populist. State utility commissions have on average become less sympathetic to the needs of investors. Therefore they are less likely than in the past to accept the decision of directors to pay out cash when a utility's finances are strapped. The prevailing conception among regulators, either dictated by state law and regulation or held as a moral presumption, has become that bondholders and preferred holders have rights to returns, but common share holders' rights to returns are not inviolate.

• The climate of litigation is pressuring directors to be more cautious. Should they pay common dividends too long (in the 20/20 hindsight of lawyers), and then omit preferred payments, directors and managements are more likely to be sued and/or removed than in the past. Thus there is a stronger bias to cut or omit common payments to protect the corporate assets for senior holders. In the same way, lenders no longer accept the "necessity" of paying the common holders at the accustomed rate when working out loan terms with utility managements. Such payments are now viewed as highly discretionary.

• The scale of problems in the electric utility business has increased, particularly where nuclear power plants (with a huge minimum unit of investment at risk) and environmental issues are at stake. An adverse regulatory or court ruling with major impact on cash flows is more likely than in the past. Regulators and courts tend to rule without balancing the interests of common dividend recipients. (As will be discussed elsewhere, the risks are lower in investing in natural gas distribution and transmission, although they have risen in recent years;

even lower risks have been evident if one restricted attention to dividend-paying telephone companies' common stocks.)

The investor must be vigilant for signs of danger. One must avoid tying the ego to the dollar by linking personal self-esteem with financial success alone. One must accept one's humanness and the inevitability of possible error. One must certainly recognize that fundamentals change. Therefore, when the market treats a specific stock adversely (i.e, out of line with its group), there is a reason. The investor must learn that reason promptly, and evaluate it—and be totally prepared to act. Wishing it away or ignoring it is a prescription for pain and trouble in the form of lost capital, reduced income, and psychological tension and confusion over one's portfolio.

Key to loss avoidance is anticipation. All too often investors are lulled into the comfort of hindsight. The evening news, the early-morning TV investment/business shows, and the daily press all fill our minds with explanations of what has already happened. The tendency is to accept such a sequence (an event followed by a 20/20 hindsight explanation) as one's lot in investment life. We are subtly drawn into a mental pattern of taking our lumps, hearing the now-obvious explanation, and mumbling "Oh, yeah, I should have known that would happen." The better, i.e., successful, way to invest is to attempt to *anticipate events by examining the realistic possibilities in advance.* Major consulting firms refer to this by such terms as scenario analysis. The object, especially for the loss-averse utility-oriented investor, is to spot problems before they come to roost, and to step aside prudently. Thus, for example, one must give up the siren song of the high current dividend yield *before* the dividend is cut (or, worse yet, omitted), in order to avoid capital loss.

The greater one's degree of risk aversion, the less forgiving one must be. It is usually most prudent to accept a small loss and move capital to a less risky situation. If one lets sentimental attachment to a stock, or the glories of past history, or ego, or the small cost of a selling commission prevent any decision to sell, losses are likely to follow. The investor must always remain cool, calculating, and rational. The principle that loss avoidance comes first in conservative investing must govern the hold/sell decision.

In chapter 14, which reveals a master signal system, a matrix outlines decision rules for buying, holding, and selling based on trends in dividend payments. A basic principle is that any adverse signal from the board of directors (such as a break in the pattern of increases, or a deceleration of increases) is not a random event and should be heeded as if the change in policy were a deliberate signal. Sometimes an investor can also project possible distress to the common dividend stream by watching the pattern of payout ratios. This can be a very useful early indicator.

The payout ratio can be calculated in various ways. Preferred dividends can be included, but doing so will reduce sensitivity to the changes observed over time. Cash flow can be used rather than earnings alone, but in that approach capital spending should also be considered since it is a major use of funds. For the armchair individual investor, simply the percentage of dividends per common share to EPS is a useful guide and one easily calculated. If this relationship creeps higher, even while payments per share are still being raised, there is cause for concern. Unless earnings improve from internal cost cutting, or unless rate relief is granted, the pot of gold from which dividend checks are paid will prove limited. It is important to remember that utilities are by definition leveraged businesses and that the common shareholder's payment is at the low end of the spectrum (Figure 10.1).

Often the market will require a higher yield from companies whose payout ratios are rising or already high. This reflects the collective judgment of investors that all may not be well despite the continued favorable actions of directors. The investor holding such a stock must guard against the temptation to consider the now high yield a friend and comforter. One tends to think, "Yes, but the high yield will keep the stock from falling any further." Quite the contrary: history shows that high yields reflect real fundamental problems that often—too often for the conservative investor to tolerate—foretell later cuts or omissions in common payouts. So a high yield should act as a strong caution flag rather than a comfort source. As shown in the next chapter, over the past ten years there is nearly a 100% perfect record for adverse dividend actions (omissions or reductions) within 12 months by the stocks which display the highest current yields.

Figure 10.1 History of High Payout Ratios by Philadelphia Electric Co.				
Year	$ Div.	$ EPS	Pct. Payout	Avg. Yield
1974	1.64	1.81	91%	11.4%
1975	1.64	1.86	88	12.3
1976	1.64	1.81	86	10.0
1977	1.76	1.87	94	9.2
1978	1.80	1.87	96	10.3
1979	1.80	1.86	97	11.5
1980	1.80	2.00	90	12.7
1981	1.90	2.25	84	14.8
1982	2.06	2.39	86	13.5
1983	2.12	2.40	88	13.4
1984	2.20	2.70	81	17.6
1985	2.20	2.56	86	14.0
1986	2.20	2.39	85	10.7
1987	2.20	2.33	94	10.4
1988	2.20	2.33	94	11.5
1989	2.20	2.36	93	10.1
1990	1.45	0.58	250	7.6
1991	1.225	2.15	57	5.6
1992	1.325	1.90	70	5.4

An injury suffered by the utilities investor due to poor stock selection or stubbornness in holding a deteriorating issue hurts twice: current yield is reduced or wiped out and capital is also impaired. The current cash return can be reasonably fully replaced, but capital lost is difficult to rebuild without taking on risky investments. Therefore the conservative investor should do everything possible to avoid suffering the double blow of a dividend cut or omission. Remember at all times that dividends are no longer sacred and that a troubled stock will not usually heal itself quickly. Step aside and seek safety and a secure return elsewhere!

Suppose you are made privy to a certain investment formula for dealing with utility stocks. The formula is designed to choose, once per year, two stocks for investment for income. Suppose the formula produced the following actual results, year by year:

OUTCOME OF DIVIDEND STREAM IN FOLLOWING YEARS		
YEAR-END	STOCK A	STOCK B
1981	cut '84	omit '90
1982	cut '86	cut 84, omit '85
1983	cut '84, omit 86	omit '84
1984	omit '85	cut '85
1985	omit '86	cut '86
1986	cut '87, omit '90	cut '87
1987	cut '88	already cut '87
1988	cut '89, omit '90	omit '90
1989	omit '90	omit '90
1990	cut '91	already cut '90

Would you follow this system for selecting income investments? If you have ever bought a utility stock on the recommendation of a broker (or after running the numbers yourself) because the stock offered one of the highest yields available, you have been following this system! It is a formula for disaster. It works much better as a means of selecting short-sale candidates than as a way of buying secure investments.

Now you are about to be given the details of the formula or system that produced the above results. It is simply as follows:

- As of December 31, rank all electric utility common stocks according to their indicated yield (latest quarterly dividend annualized, divided by current market price).

- Buy the stock with the highest (Stock A) and second-highest (Stock B) yields on the list.

Chasing the highest current yield over the past decade would have produced the sorry results above. For those who want the details, the following is a list of the names of Stocks A and B. As they say, "you can look it up."

IDENTITY OF STOCKS QUALIFYING UNDER SYSTEM		
YEAR-END	STOCK A	STOCK B
1981	Bangor Hydro-Electric	Ohio Edison
1982	Duquesne Light	CMS Energy
1983	P S of Indiana	Long Island Ltg.
1984	CMS Energy	Central Maine Pw.
1985	NIPSCO	Kansas Gas & El.
1986	Niagara Mowawk Pwr.	Centerior
1987	Central Hudson G&E	Centerior
1988	Pinnacle West	P S of New Mexico
1989	Tucson Electric	Pinnacle West
1990	Eastern Util Assoc	Ohio Edison
1991	TNP Enterprises	Nevada Power

Almost like clockwork, each year since 1983 the single electric utility with the highest yield has cut or omitted its dividend within the following 12 months. And the second-highest yielder? If it had not already cut its dividend (as in the cases of year-end 1987 and 1990), in every case from 1983 through 1990 that company also would reduce or omit its dividend in the next 12 months.

One lesson that the above information should teach is that the market is not stupid; since the utilities area is well researched and heavily followed by professional institutional investors, there are relatively few major surprises—especially among large-capitalization issues. The collective wisdom of investors, in attaching to certain stocks the caution flag of an unusually high yield, is well founded: those stocks are quite likely to be the ones cutting or omitting dividends.

The data show a similar pattern if one looks beyond the top one or two and at the 10% of electric utilities with the highest yields each year-end. Thinking in terms of a "failure rate" for a manufactured product, here are the results (with failure defined as a dividend cut or omission):

| | PERCENT FAILED WITHIN | |
YEAR-END	3 YEARS	LONGER
1981	27	64
1982	44	82
1983	64	82
1984	56	82
1985	56	91
1986	64	82
1987	64	82
1988	73	
1989	64	

If you were a manufacturing plant manager and your production facility produced items intended for robust, long service lives, and the actual failure rates were as above, you would make some radical changes to your methods as quickly as possible. Unfortunately, too many utility investors make the mistake of continuing to select their stocks by exactly this same old and proven (disastrous!) method: chasing high current yield. The odds are strongly stacked against them, as shown above.

This system has made some eerily accurate predictions. Consolidated Edison Company of New York, the first electric to omit its dividend in some decades when its directors did so in April 1974, was in the top decile of high yielders at year-end 1973 (and 1972)! And General Public Utilities, ill-fated operator of Three Mile Island, was on the list in 1979! Public Service Company of New Hampshire, whose Seabrook nuclear facility eventually drove it to a Chapter 11 bankruptcy, was in the top 10% at year-ends 1980 through 1983 before omitting its dividend in 1984. The other prominent Chapter 11 case in the industry, El Paso Electric, stopped raising its dividend in 1987, ranked in the 10% of highest yielders at December 1988, and omitted its dividend in 1989.

The undaunted optimist might note that arguably 30% to 40% of the highest-yielding stocks do not cut or omit their dividends (at least, not within one year) and therefore there is a chance to win with the high-yield strategy. For the conservative and serious investor, such an attitude is the equivalent of playing Russian roulette, or playing with fire. In this case, the fire will not only damage the investor's income stream but will also consume part of his or her capital at the same time.

In most recent years, the apparent current yield of the highest-yield utility stocks has been only a few percent above the average yield for all utilities paying dividends. The added risk is simply not worth the marginal income. Without going through complex mathematics, it works like this: suppose you can get a 6% cash yield on a good-quality utility stock that is raising its dividend annually. As an alternative, you are considering buying a higher-risk utility with a 10% cash yield. Suppose there is a 50% chance that the latter company will cut its dividend, say by 40% in the next year (see the tables above).

If that happens, your cash return on cost will turn out to be 6% anyway, but your capital will be impaired when the stock reacts to the dividend cut. A 50% chance of a 40% dividend cut implies a 50% chance of a loss in price (albeit perhaps not as much as 40%). Even if the stock declines only 20% on the bad news, the expected value of that loss is 10%, which will wipe out the entire 10% return you think you are buying, and which will swamp the 4% difference in current cash yield you are seeking by playing the high-current-yield game. This comparison favors the lower-yield issue even further when one realizes that its chance of actual capital appreciation is greater because its dividend is rising.

While the tables in this chapter focus on results from electric (and combined gas and electric) companies, similar results are found if one examines natural gas transmission and distribution stocks.

There have been numerous dividend cuts in those groups as well. Gas utility stocks must be studied on a separate yield scale from electric companies' shares: a high yield among the former often looks like a medium yield among the latter. As of this writing, water and telephone stocks have generally avoided dividend cuts and omissions. However, owners should be vigilant, using the "relative-yield" technique detailed in Chapter 19.

The good news for careful investors determined to play a game with the odds on their side is this: it is not even necessary to wait for a utility stock to arrive on the list of the 10% most likely to fail. There is, fortunately, an early warning signal in almost every case. And that signal is the failure of the board of directors to raise the dividend as in the past. A zero-growth dividend is an early sign of potential trouble. Selling the stock on this seemingly mild piece of bad news will be cheap insurance against further price erosion and possible dividend reductions or omissions later. As the old investment adage has it, the first loss is the best loss! Why? Because the first bad news is seldom the only bad news.

The predictive value of the flat-line or zero-growth dividend is so important that it is one of the six critical signals in the system for utility investors. This is developed more fully in Chapters 14 and 15.

The lesson of this chapter: the only sensible choice for the serious investor (as contrasted with the thrill seeker) is to invest for total return, not for maximum current income, from utility common stocks.

Those who are ignorant of the lessons of history, we are told, are doomed to relearn those lessons. The purpose of this chapter is to impress on the reader indelibly the terrible financial results that follow from chasing high yield in utility stocks. While of course past results cannot be taken as a guaranteed predictor of future performance, the pattern that the past decade has presented is so clear as to convince any reasonable observer that choosing utility stocks based on high current yield is not the way to achieve either high yield or peace of mind. Rather, it appears a high-percentage way to reduce one's capital and fail to receive a decent current yield on one's investments.

This chapter will present vignettes of individual high-yield utility stocks from the decade prior to publication of the book. The methodology is slightly different from that in the previous chapter, in two ways. First, the stocks named here are included regardless of whether they had already reduced their dividends at the time they rose to the highest-yield rank among their peers. Second, this chapter seeks to make the result of investing in individual high-yield issues less abstract, by dealing not in averages of the 10 worst, but rather by following the actual histories of one individual stock per year.

It should be remembered that the approach used in this and the previous chapter is to take a snapshot of yields once a year, at year-end. One could rank all utilities on any given market date and would certainly have identified other risky situations by looking on June 30 or some other date. In some cases those stocks had deeply cut or omitted dividends by December 31, already slashing their yields, and therefore are not included in the following discussion. While the author has not performed computer screening to demonstrate the investment results if one bought the highest-yielding utility at, say, each month's or quarter's end, it is safe to say that the results would be every bit as disastrous as what follows.

Typically, for reasons discussed elsewhere in the book, shares of electric utilities tend to trade at prices producing higher current yields than do those of gas systems, telephones, or water companies. Therefore, except in the case of extreme distress for a company in those other areas, some electric utility will usually earn the unfortunate distinction of selling at the highest apparent yield. The year-by-year examples in this chapter center on electric utilities.

However, the principle of avoiding the highest yielders can be applied equally in the other groups. The electrics were chosen for discussion here because they are more numerous and each year in fact produced at least one dividend cut or omission. In the late 1980s and early 1990s adverse dividend actions among gas companies were on a sharp upswing. So far, telephone and water companies have escaped unscathed. That does not mean, of course, that their dividends will remain sacrosanct in the future. Be ever watchful no matter what kinds of utility shares you own.

1982

The highest-yielding utility stock on December 31, 1981, was Bangor Hydro-Electric. Its closing price was $10.00. Therefore, its indicated annual dividend rate of $1.52 per share provided at the time a current cash yield of 15.2%.

Bangor Hydro represents a relative success story among the high-yielders of the 1982-1992 period. Why? It did not cut its dividend immediately in the following year. In fact, small further increases in the annual rate continued, and the maximum paid out reached $1.60 per share in 1984. But the market already sensed something was wrong at the end of 1981 by demanding a high cash return of BANG. Perhaps contributing to the high yield was a bit of market inefficiency: the stock traded over the counter and the company had only about four million shares outstanding, rendering it less than appealing to many institutions and therefore probably keeping its price a bit below what a larger, listed company in similar circumstances would have commanded.

The market could see clearly that the dividend was in trouble. The stock fell to a low price of $5.50 in 1984, cutting the investor's capital by 45%. In the first quarter of 1985, directors cut the dividend in half, to an annual rate of $0.80 per share. Clearly, the market—that is, the collective opinion of participants in the stock—had already well discounted the cut. In fact, it appears that an even more drastic action by directors had been expected. The stock, contrary to the common pattern, actually had hit its low *before* the dividend cut.

By late 1985 and certainly throughout most of 1986, the year following the dividend cut, the stock could have been sold at $10 or higher, finally restoring the original investment of those who reached for the highest yield at the end of 1981.

Dividends, however, have been a different story. As of early 1993 the annual rate had been gradually restored only to a $1.32 level. Thus the end-of-1981 investor has yet to receive again the $1.52 per share that seemed so tempting at the start of 1982. As indicated earlier, BANG was actually one of the *less painful* of the stories in this chapter!

1983

Another New England company, as events would have it, was the bad-luck story of 1983 for investors who chased the highest current yield on December 31, 1982. Fitchburg Gas & Electric, a small-city company located in north-central Massachusetts, was the stock. At the end of 1982 its shares closed at $19.25 on the American Stock Exchange. The $2.60 annual dividend yielded an apparently irresistible 13.5% at that price.

FG&E was the earliest casualty of the brewing fiasco north of the New Hampshire border. The company owned a tiny piece of the Seabrook nuclear power project and for that reason was forced to contribute its share to mounting construction costs and to endure delays that history would show had barely begun by 1983. Those delays meant interest on borrowed funds, no return on the capital invested, and angry regulators.

The company was able to get through 1983 with the dividend intact, and its stock has slipped only slightly, to $18.75, by year-end. But that would prove of small consolation by mid-1984, when directors omitted payments altogether. Thus, FG&E as a high-yield situation took 18 months to failure. The stock price was battered, reaching its low of $6.875 during 1985. The investor's reward for chasing high yield was at that point a 64.3% capital loss—and for the present a zero income stream.

The price did recover during 1986 to the end-of-1982 level, benefiting those who had the courage to hold on when it was at $7 and paying nothing. The company never did fully restore the $2.60 dividend rate: it reached $2.12 annually in 1991 before the directors agreed to an acquisition by UNITIL, based in, ironically, New Hampshire. FG&E was the first of many former high yielders that have not yet fully delivered again the dividends investors could not resist in prior years.

1984

Public Service of Indiana, which has since changed its name to PSI Resources, was the highest-yielding stock as of December 31, 1983. By all accounts, investors should have known better than to buy or hold it. All that was necessary was to follow the wise investment dictum that what looks too good to be true, *is*. At the end of 1983 PIN was yielding, at least apparently, 23.66% from its $2.82 indicated annual dividend rate. The price was $11.875 on New Year's eve. A bargain? Hardly, as would quickly become obvious.

In the first quarter of 1984, directors slashed the dividend rate to $1.00 per share, a drop of over 64%. The stock continued falling, and at the end of 1984 was a mere $7.00 per share. One-year result for the investor who reached for high yield: just a dollar of income rather than $2.82, and a capital depletion of 41%. Not exactly what conservative investors had bargained for.

The bad news was not finished, however. The dividend was omitted entirely in the first quarter of 1986. Again, analysts had apparently seen this coming, as the stock's low price had already been touched at $6.875. That was down some 79% from the stock's 1982 high of over $33 when its dividend growth rate had been reduced to zero. (In Chapter 15 flat-line dividends will be shown to be an important selling signal.) A class-action shareholder suit was later settled in favor of the plaintiffs, with the allegation being failure by management to fully disclose the company's problems in a timely manner.

Once the worst news, namely the omission, was out of the way, the stock was able to start recovering. By late in 1986 it could be sold for more than the end-of-1983 price. But dividends have yet to be restored significantly. By late 1992 the annual rate was back up to just $1.00. Even a merger proposal in early 1993 left the shares well below their 1982 high when dividend growth had ceased.

1985

The top-yield spot at the end of 1984 would return to a New England company, and in fact it was to be proven another casualty of Seabrook. Maine Public Service closed the year at $12.25 after having recently reduced its annual dividend rate from $2.32 to $1.40 per share. Even the reduced rate offered an 11.4% apparent yield. The stock was already down from a high over $28 in 1983, when it had paid $2.22 per share in total. Those watching relative yield—the movement of a utility stock relative to peers in terms of current yield—had already been tipped off to trouble brewing. The problem was allowance for funds used during construction or AFUDC. This is an accounting term that, put simply, allows companies to report earnings that are not real cash earnings. A utility can't very long pay dividends when AFUDC makes up a lot of its reported earnings.

MAP, which traded then (as now) on the American Stock Exchange, omitted its dividend entirely in early 1985, providing rapid negative feedback for those who chased high yield at the prior year's end. As noted above, the stock had already been badly pounded and was trading below book value. It moved to a low of $11.00 per share in 1985 and started to recover. Partial dividend restoration later that year certainly helped speed the process. In an unusual pattern caused by the exceptionally rapid restoration of dividends, MAP stock could actually be sold at its pre-omission price again in the same year.

Maine Public Service is the least unhappy of the stories in this chapter. It is the only one to have restored fully its dividend to the pre-trouble level—the only company out of a decade's highest yielders! That restoration occurred in 1988. The shares were actually split 2:1 in 1989 and the company now pays $1.76 annually, which would be $3.52 on the old stock. But the road from $28 down to $11 and back up to $29, with a dividend cut and omission on the way, was rougher than a utility investor should ever have bargained to experience.

1986

Action swung back to the midwest the next year, and the top of the high-yield list at December 31, 1985, was held by Northern Indiana Public Service, now called NIPSCO Industries. The stock ended the year at $9.875, and its $1.56 annual dividend rate seemed to offer a 15.8% yield. The income stream was to last only three more quarters, however, as directors omitted the fourth-quarter payout entirely. Already down from an earlier-1980s high over $32, the shares had little downside left by the time the omission occurred. Bad regulatory news continued to follow the company due to opposition to its nuclear project, and the stock finally bottomed at $8.00 per share in 1987—75% off its high.

The bad news was not too devastating for investors in NIPSCO— the stock was off barely 20% from its already-depressed prices at year end 1985. And the $9.875 buy price could have been recouped in 1987. But the $1.56 dividend stream remains at least partially a mirage: although payments were resumed after a short period, the rate at the end of 1992 had been restored only to $1.32 per share—still not what the high yield seekers at the end of 1985 thought they were bargaining for.

1987

Niagara Mohawk Power took the dubious honors at the end of trading in December 1986: its then dividend rate of $2.08 per share represented an alluring 12.4% on the stock's year-closing price of $16.75. And for a time investors thought they were beating the odds. Despite ongoing problems at the Nine Mile Point nuclear project, the dividend was temporarily continued at the $2.08 rate.

But in the third quarter of 1987, NMK's directors slashed the dividend by 42% to just $1.20 per share. The stock closed the year at $12.125, meaning that instead of a 12.4% return the investor earned a negative 17.8% total return in the 12 months. This was during the year of the great stock market crash of October. Despite that one-day 508-point disaster, the Dow-Jones Industrial Average was only a slight loser for the year, compared with the 17.8% loss in NMK.

The bad news was not finished yet, however. Troubles at Nine Mile continued, and directors in the third quarter of 1989 omitted the common dividend to Niagara Mohawk's share-holders entirely. The stock touched a low of $10.75 in 1989 before starting its recovery. (Once again, note that the low in price was reached shortly after the dividend omission!) At that point, the high-yield investor had suffered a capital loss of nearly 36% and was receiving zero income.

The stock did not recover to its starting point of $16.75 until 1991. And the dividend, only now being repaired, was back up to just $0.80 per share—not even 40% of the old rate, by early 1993. While the stock had recovered to the $19 area, the ride had been rough and the total return was well below what the income investor envisioned at the start.

1988

Bad news came in clusters for New York State utility investors: the unfortunate distinction of offering the highest apparent yield at December 31, 1987, went to Central Hudson Gas & Electric, another of the victims of trouble in getting Nine Mile Point on line and into the rate base. At the end of 1987, CNH's annual dividend rate, most recently declared at $2.96, represented a suspiciously high 17.2% yield on the $17.25 closing stock price. The directors had signaled future trouble by going to a no-growth dividend policy, and the stock had started to reflect danger by having already declined from its 1986 high of $39.875 per share. Institutional ownership had dwindled to an unusually low 9%.

The $2.96 rate was already history: in the very first quarter of 1988 the board slashed it to $1.70 per share—a 42% cut, parallel to that made earlier by the Niagara Mohawk directors. Apparently, investors had already expected roughly such a cut, since the stock's bottom price was $16.875. By the end of the year it could be sold at $21.50 as interest rates fell sharply in the aftermath of the 1987 crash.

As of early 1993, the dividend rate had been restored to just $2.00 per share—still almost a third less than investors bargained for more than five years earlier.

1989

The scene shifted from the Rust Belt and the northeast and to the southwest. The fallout from overexpansion in the wake of formerly high energy prices had begun to catch up with the Texas/Oklahoma/Colorado/New Mexico/Arizona area. The highest apparent yield on December 31, 1988, belonged to Pinnacle West Capital, based in Phoenix. The company had changed its name from Arizona Public Service and had diversified out of its familiar business into banking and land development. Both would prove nearly fatal errors.

By the end of 1988, PNW had already cut its dividend rate from $2.80 to $1.60 per share. The stock was down from a high of $32.25 to just $15.875—already a drop of just over 50%. The yield of 10% from even the already-reduced dividend was to prove a mirage in the southwestern desert, however.

In the fourth quarter of 1989, PNW directors omitted the common dividend. As the national banking crisis deepened and western real estate values started to crack, PNW stock plummeted all the way to $5. Again, in the same year of the omission, the price low was hit. The stock closed the year at $11.00. Instead of getting a 10% cash yield, investors had seen their last dividend checks and were still facing nearly a 31% loss of capital in the twelve months—if they'd had the nerve to hang on at $6 and $5 when the word *bankruptcy* was being used freely in the press.

A price recovery to the end-of-1988 level did occur in 1990. But that was of only partial solace to investors, who have yet to see any dividends since their last checks in 1989 as of this writing.

1990

The new decade brought even worse news for another utility based in Arizona. Highest-yield "honors" went to Tucson Electric Power, which had already reduced its payout from $3.90 per share to just $1.60 in the third quarter of 1989. At $18.00, the shares seemed to offer a yield of 8.9%—well above the industry average as interest rates continued falling. Note that this was already a badly fallen angel: the stock had careened southward from a high of $65 in 1987 when dividend growth stopped!

Was TEP a bargain yet? Far from it. It took only one quarter for investors to be slapped on the other cheek: the $1.60 dividend did not last past the next directors' meeting. Payments were completely omitted. The company had about 50% excess capacity coming on line and populist-thinking state regulators had made it clear the new coal-fired capacity, on top of TEP's partial stake in PNW's Palo Verde nukes, would not be put into the rate base. The company's chairman resigned suddenly.

The stock sank to a sickening $5.375 per share by the end of 1990, representing a 70% capital loss as the reward for those who had thought just 12 months earlier that the dividend cut to $1.60 was the worst of the news. As of this writing, there has been no price move remotely close to $18 so far; in fact, in late 1992 the shares briefly traded at a new low of $1.00—a nearly 98% capital loss from the company's glory days. Talk of a bankruptcy filing had died down, but prospects for any dividends still seemed well off into the future. Think of it: the stock's *price* had fallen to less than what its annual *dividend* had been just 36 months earlier. In mid-December 1992, the company "restructured" $2.3 billion of debt, leases, and preferred stock by issuing

135 million new common shares, flooding the market with stock in the hands of former creditors. While a formal bankruptcy has been averted, revenue per share is now about $3 per year, indicating little near-future prospect of resuming dividends at any level.

1991

The scene shifted back to Massachusetts. The distinction of offering the seemingly highest yield at December 31, 1990, belonged to Eastern Utilities Associates. This fairly small company was among a handful of local bidders trying to rescue its own financial involvements with the ill-fated Seabrook plant. Its aggressive strategy was to buy the bankruptcy estate of the project's manager and principal owner, Public Service Company of New Hampshire.

At the end of 1990, EUA was trading at $24, and its latest dividend rate was $2.60 per share, indicating an apparent yield of 10.8% at a time when average-risk utilities offered cash dividends in the 7.5% range. The yield was to prove unsustainable as the financial pinch on EUA became too much to allow continuing the old dividend rate. Readers will remember from Chapter 10 that dividends are no longer sacred: EUA was far from the first distressed New England utility to throw in the dividend towel.

The scenario played out with an unusual twist. For the second quarter the directors "deferred" the dividend, meaning they didn't omit it but didn't pay it either. In their next meeting they paid $0.12 per share for the prior quarter and cut the new rate from $0.65 to just $0.34 per share—over a 47% reduction in shareholders' income stream. The stock hit a low of $15.75 in 1991, representing a drop of 34% from the year's start and some 62% from its 1989 high.

As of the end of 1992 the dividend had not yet been increased from its more humble $1.36 annual rate, and the stock was trading in the $22-23 range—still representing a small capital loss for those who had the intestinal fortitude to hold through the dip below $16. Once again, chasing high yield had proved a quick route to losses. A positive postscript: in early 1993 the rate was improved to $1.44.

Shift the scene back to the Southwestern Sunbelt. At the end of 1991 the highest-yielding electric utility common stock was TNP Enterprises, whose operating subsidiary was Texas-New Mexico Power. The dividend, which had just been flat-lined at $1.63 annually, offered a yield of nearly 8.5% when middle-quality companies were trading to yield about 6%.

The jury is still out on TNP as of this writing. The company did take advantage of low interest rates in 1992 to refinance some of its high-cost debt. That has reduced its financial pinch some-what. But earnings were barely covering the dividend rate as of late 1992 (the payout ratio was in the dangerous area around 90%).

While the dividend was maintained through 1992, the history of the past 10 years seemed to bode no good for holders of TNP. If it is to be able to hold the dividend, it will be the first highest-yielder in a decade to escape the scourge. It is positioned in an area where several other companies have had financial strains and cut their payouts. Besides Pinnacle West and Tucson Electric, discussed above, Sierra Pacific in Nevada cut its dividend in 1992, and El Paso Electric, close to TNP's home, was in Chapter 11 proceedings. Public Service of New Mexico also had omitted its dividends as early as 1989. We wish the company and its share-holders well, but in our opinion the weight of the evidence seemed in early 1993 to point to higher risk than the conservative utilities investor wanted to bargain for.

1993

The latest year-end highest-yield "honors" before this book went to press belonged, once again, to TNP Enterprises. Its yield on December 31, 1992, was 8.58% . . . assuming no dividend cut. Not far behind on the highest-yield list was Centerior Energy, the combination of the former Cleveland Electric Illuminating and Toledo Edison. CX yielded 8.05% on its $1.60 annual dividend rate, but its payout ratio exceeded 100%, and its dividend had been flat since a reduction in 1988.

For those readers interested in applying the logic in the gas utility area, at the end of 1992 the highest-yielding gas company was NUI Corp., serving New Jersey. Its dividend had been raised $0.02 in 1992 after five flat years. What is of some concern is the cluster of New Jersey companies at the top of the highest-yield gas stocks list: New Jersey Resources and South Jersey Industries are also among the top four. One cannot be sure that all or any of these will reduce their dividends; the conservative investor will heed the lesson of history and bypass such names in favor of other companies with strong dividend growth and perhaps a 1% lower current yield. Examples in early 1993 included Brooklyn Union Gas and Alatenn Resources. The tradeoff is good insurance.

There you have it. A decade of nasty surprises for utility investors who fell into the trap of buying the highest-yield stocks. It should be added that there is a slow trap into which existing holders also fall. As a stock declines in price, its existing dividend rate begins to provide a higher and higher yield. The holder is seduced into thinking, "I can't sell it way down here . . . look, the yield is so high!" As we have seen, the dividend in such cases too often becomes a thing of the past, and with it the stock's price. It is terribly important for the investor planning for a secure retirement to retain his or her capital. Will Rogers is reported to have said he was more concerned with the return *of* his capital than the return *on* his capital. Amen to that.

Now you have seen the evidence of recent history. Take care to use the lessons it teaches, without first paying the price of relearning them.

PART THREE

OVERVIEW: YOU AND UTILITY INVESTING

CURRENT CASH OR TOTAL RETURN? ALWAYS GO FOR QUALITY!

Investors who buy stocks for the dividend income should consider the total package of risk and reward more carefully than they often seem to do. It is tempting to buy common stocks whose latest year's dividends represent a high percentage of the current stock price. The buyer believes that this high apparent yield will continue. What is often not fully considered is this: the collective wisdom and expectations among all knowledgeable market players set current stock prices, so an apparently high yield is commonly a sign of generally perceived high risk. Thus, the buyer of a high-yield stock is taking two risks: first, that the dividend itself may be reduced or omitted, and second, that the stock's price would almost certainly decline if such an adverse dividend action occurred.

Most times since the great depression of the 1930s, common stocks have tended to provide lower current (cash) yields than have either long-term bonds or preferred stocks. In this environment, if an investor truly requires a high current yield, he or she should seek it in those senior instruments. They are less likely than common shares to suffer reduced or omitted income payments, and they usually carry various covenants that promise to make up the back cash returns in the future if those unhappy events do transpire. If an income-oriented buyer has a serious need for maximum current income, he or she has no business taking the incremental risks in common-stock ownership and therefore should restrict activities to senior securities. This posture is perhaps more psychologically appropriate following retirement, but may not be financially necessary even then, if a sufficient asset pool has been amassed by that time so that low yields provide adequate total dollar income.

The younger buyer of utilities for income should specialize not in pure current cash income alone, but rather in total return. This term means the sum of cash return plus realized or unrealized price appreciation. That appreciation, in turn, is projected to be caused by a rising level of dividends over the years. That rate of growth, expressed as a percentage per year, may be added to the cash yield (dividend rate divided by stock price) to figure the total return. Thus, a stock currently yielding 6% whose dividend grows by 4% annually may be projected (ceteris paribus) to provide a total return of 10% per year. The actual result will vary as the company's fortunes and the market's perceptions/expectations of them change and, significantly, as tax policy and the level of prevailing interest rates shift. The early Clinton tax plan was to hold the rate on capital gains while raising the rate on dividend and interest income. This approach adds further validity to the concept of seeking capital gains from utility investments.

Major capital gains can be achieved with the use of conservative instruments such as utility common stocks in periods when interest rates are declining. On the other hand, even the best-quality among utility shares will decline, in some cases severely, in the face of wiltingly higher interest rates. Most investors in quality blue chips, and especially in utility shares, consider themselves long-term (lifetime?) holders. But because of the major influence of interest-rate cycles, it is suggested that a policy of riding the interest-rate cycle be pursued (see Chapter 18). Thus, even quality stocks bought allegedly primarily for income should also be viewed as subject to sale to capture capital appreciation—and, probably more importantly, to avoid cyclical capital loss. So, even for investors whose stated strategy is a long-term "buy and hold" on quality issues, the subject of selling should not be ignored.

This chapter opened with the assertion of the theory that total return is the way to go in investing for income, at least before retirement occurs. This position makes intuitive sense since the

highest-yield securities—whether commons, preferreds, or bonds
—by their nature involve above-average risk, and therefore
avoiding them puts the investor in the position of "sticking with
quality." But more than theory backs this position. Actual results
support this approach.

REACHING FOR HIGH YIELD: THE HIDDEN KILLER

We have made the point that one of the critical ingredients of
building wealth is avoiding losses. This is an especially important
lesson for conservative investors such as those investing in utilities. The reason is that such investors have a smaller chance to
"hit a home run" in the next investment after "striking out" on a
prior try. That is because, by its nature, investing and wealth
building via a conservative route such as utilities means there will
be no unusually huge winners chosen—no early MCIs or Amgens
or McDonald's. Because the types of stocks the investor will be
buying offer little likelihood of unusual success, extra care must
be taken to assure that the smallest possible degree of risk is
taken. In investing in a "conservative" type of industry such as
utilities, the investor is psychologically prone to an error of
projection: what has worked successfully in the past *seems* very
likely—more likely than is actually the case—to continue in the
future. A utility stock, in the naive investor's mind at least, is
rock solid because:

- They have paid dividends without fail for the last
  umpteen years; and

- No matter how bad things get, "they can't turn out the
  lights."

Unfortunately, these observations are not relevant to the central
question for the utility investor. And that question is, how secure
and how likely to grow is the income stream *from today forward?*

A long record of uninterrupted dividends is only as relevant as a
long record of not having bounced a check: if something bad
happens tomorrow or next month, all the good history and the
best of intentions may mean the streak of success could suddenly
end! And the observation that electric power (or natural gas
service, or telephone communications) is a necessity does not

imply that the stream of common dividends is as secure as the provision of the utility service. Remember, the common shareholder stands at the back of the line in terms of rights; especially where utility commissions are either elected or populist in leaning (or both!) there is every reason to assume the worst: that in time of difficulty the common holder's needs and expectations may well be given little consideration. Perhaps because of their public sector perspective, the attitude of many regulators is less than staunchly pro-capitalist. They have often been quoted in decisions and in the press as saying that common shareholders are risk takers by nature and have no entitlement to expectation of a secure return—or any return.

So, while the utility itself will continue sending out water or power or natural gas or connecting phone calls, that does not automatically mean it will be allowed to do so at a profit, let alone at a big enough profit to continue the past record of continuous or rising dividends to common holders. Remember, the term "public utility" itself gives a clue as to the mindset of many regulators: this operation exists in large part to satisfy the needs of the public. But if times get tough, those needs will be given preference over the common shareholder's dividend check every time.

Therein lies a hidden but huge risk for the utilities investor: not only is the income stream at risk, but impairment of that flow of quarterly checks will surely carry with it a second and even worse curse: as documented in the preceding chapter, the investor's capital will be significantly impaired. And lost capital is not easily replaced when the program involves deliberately *not* taking above-average risks in search of big rewards.

THE SOLUTION: TOTAL RETURN INVESTING

As will be shown, the most universal and accurate signal that danger is present is the apparent availability of an unusually high yield. The high yield is alluring to the investor, and acts as a huge temptation for brokers. As salespeople, brokers know that they should listen to the client and then sell the client what he or she wants. That's the essence of successful, easy, low-pressure salesmanship. If you, the investor, indicate yield is the objective, very few brokers will sift among dozens of utilities and present a lower-yielding security as their choice for you. Why? The broker knows that someone else may suggest a higher-yield name, and the investor will too often buy that instead. So, in classic Gresham's-Law fashion, recommendations of lower-yielding but higher quality utility stocks will be crowded out by advice to buy higher-yielding issues that involve not-so-obvious but very real risks. *Beware the high yield!*

FOURTEEN

The point has been made that seeking total return rather than maximum current income is the key to success in utilities investing. What is required for implementing this general principle is a set of rules, or a signaling system. This chapter provides that framework for making the all-important buy/hold/sell/avoid decisions. Note that the signals to be discussed in the following pages are two sided: they cover both buying as well as selling. Just because you are a long-term investor by objective and/or by psychological bent does not mean that every individual investment you purchase will continue to merit being held until death. Far from it!

One of the truths that CD refugees who entered the stock and bond markets in 1991-1992 will inevitably discover, to their distress, is that in the stock and bond markets there is no such thing as a one-decision investment. CDs mature, relieving the holder of the decision as to whether or when to cash them in. The sell decision, so to speak, is made by the calendar's operation.

In stocks there is no such convenient nudge: the decision to hold or sell is a choice the investor must face, one that should never be made by default through paralysis, laziness, emotion, or inertia. There is no notice in the mail that you must take action or else. In Wall Street lingo: "they don't ring the bell when the move is over." It is up to the investor to exercise constant vigilance; no one has a greater incentive to take care of your money than you yourself.

115

Think of the hold/sell decision this way: each day, all of your capital is available for redeployment. Each day you do not make a decision to sell, you have actually decided to redeploy the capital exactly as it was at the prior day's market closing—without calling your broker and without paying any commissions. Therefore, while it feels less dramatic, the decision to hold is every bit as important as the decision to buy—for holding is simply buying (commission free) for another day. This is why, in the system that follows, a hold rating is generated by a specific condition, rather than being what's "left over" from all other conditions.

The theory underlying this previously undisclosed dividend-signal system has three parts:

- First, that total return rather than highest current income is the proper technique for maximizing wealth through utilities investing;

- Second, that the dividend growth rate is the critical element in total return (since it drives both the income stream and thereby the market value of the assets), and therefore the growth rate must be watched carefully; and

- Third, that the Board of Directors is in the best position to know the likely future of the corporation, and therefore the signals it provides to the investor in the form of shifts in dividend policy are extremely important.

Any utility stock—telephone, gas, water, or electric—can be associated with, or categorized by, the latest dividend signal its Board of Directors has provided. As a shorthand notation, in this chapter the following terms will be used:

DIVIDEND TREND CONDITION

CONDITION 1: STEADY GROWTH

CONDITION 2: DECELERATED GROWTH

CONDITION 3: FLAT LINE

CONDITION 4: RATE CUT

CONDITION 5: OMISSION

CONDITION 6: ACCELERATION/RESTART

These six conditions are arranged in a sequence corresponding to their most common real-world order (although not every company will necessarily always pass through *every* step in sequence). Taking an extremely long-term scenario view, one might think of the succession of conditions as a cycle exhibited by the dividend that reflects an underlying full circle of corporate health: things go along smoothly for a while; a problem develops and may become a crisis; action is taken to restore health; health is restored, growth returns and proceeds for a time; things go along smoothly . . .

One might suppose, on first glance, that conditions 1, 2, and 6 are favorable and that 3, 4, and 5 are unfavorable. In fact, as evidence from the past has tended to demonstrate, condition 2 is all too often a precursor of condition 3 or 4. Therefore, for the sake of safety, condition 2 is viewed as a negative signal. Even though some growth in the dividend rate is maintained, a cautionary signal is being sent out by the directors and should not be ignored. There are always other stocks available that are in more favorable phases of the cycle. Therefore, only conditions 6 and 1 reflect clearly healthy underlying corporate fundamentals (and even condition 1 can be misleadingly happy if the payout ratio is rising toward or has exceeded 100%).

In a slowly developing cycle, the full sequence can occur:

$$1 \longrightarrow 2 \longrightarrow 3 \longrightarrow 4 \longrightarrow 5 \longrightarrow 6 \longrightarrow 1 \ldots$$

But the investor should not assume that all six phases will occur in a neat, preprogrammed fashion. Quite often the sequence of underlying corporate fundamentals can prompt directors to bypass one or even two steps in the full cycle. This is a very important reason why it is advisable to move out of the utility stock at the very first negative signal. Most often that signal will be a condition 2 or 3. Seldom does a company go from condition 1 directly to condition 4 (let alone 5). But the conservative investor wants to take no chances of being at risk by leaving capital on the table to be swept over the investment waterfall in case a condition 4 or 5 should occur. That is why selling is required under the master signal system in either condition 2 or 3, as an insurance policy.

Sometimes, if circumstances move negatively more quickly or if the board has been overly optimistic or overly generous despite fundamental problems for the company that have been building up, the deceleration phase can be skipped over:

$$1 \longrightarrow \qquad 3 \longrightarrow 4 \longrightarrow 5 \longrightarrow 6 \longrightarrow 1 \ldots$$

Or, in more severe cases, it is possible to see the very negative condition 4 signal come despite absence of the prior warning of condition 3. This pattern can also occur if directors have been "whistling in the dark" (raising the payout ratio by declaring increases while earnings plateau or actually fall off for more than weather-related reasons):

$$1 \longrightarrow 2 \longrightarrow \qquad 4 \longrightarrow 5 \longrightarrow 6 \longrightarrow 1 \ldots$$

Sometimes, again depending on how sudden or how desperate the company's problems, an omission can occur without the prior warning of a decrease:

$$1 \longrightarrow 2 \longrightarrow 3 \longrightarrow \qquad 5 \longrightarrow 6 \longrightarrow 1 \ldots$$

In some cases, such as a negative but noncatastrophic rate decision, an omission never occurs, but a dividend reduction is necessary to align payouts with earning power. Future growth resumes from the lower base:

$$1 \longrightarrow 2 \longrightarrow 3 \longrightarrow 4 \longrightarrow \qquad 6 \longrightarrow 1 \ldots$$

On a relatively few occasions, directors will have anticipated serious trouble by decelerating growth or instituting a no-growth dividend policy. Through a well-managed process of recovery, dividend growth may be reestablished without the terrible interim shocks of a cut or omission:

$$1 \longrightarrow 2 \longrightarrow 3 \longrightarrow \qquad\qquad 6 \longrightarrow 1 \ldots$$

or merely:

$$1 \longrightarrow 2 \longrightarrow \qquad\qquad 6 \longrightarrow 1 \ldots$$

or perhaps:

$$1 \longrightarrow \qquad 3 \longrightarrow \qquad\qquad 6 \longrightarrow 1 \ldots$$

Note that for such less drastic patterns to occur generally takes several years' time. The investor following the signal system would be on the sidelines with capital protected once a condition 2 or condition 3 occurs. This would spare the risk of a condition 4 or 5 in all but extremely unusual (crisis) conditions.

Investment markets are complex milieux. One of the most baffling aspects of the markets to millions of investors for many generations has been the fact that success comes from *not* doing what seems obvious. The reason for this paradox is that the market has a tendency to anticipate future conditions and to begin to discount them before actual changed facts become common knowledge. What seems most obvious will often turn out to be unprofitable. Why? The investor paid a high price for a "proven growth stock," such as IBM, and then the company's fortunes turned soft. Or, turning to the other extreme, the utility investor's perception of the obvious action when a dividend is omitted— SELL!—usually will prove tactically 100% wrong. As will be shown, the startling truth is that the absolute best time to buy a utility stock is when the dividend has been omitted. True, and yet totally counter-intuitive. Therefore, surprising as it may seem, while Condition 5 (dividend omission) reflects a fundamental corporate crisis, it represents a buying opportunity for the sophisticated investor who capitalizes on a psychological crisis in the stock market. So, in the end, three conditions of the six are positive investment action indicators, and three are negatives:

DIVIDEND TREND CONDITION	Fundamentally:	Signal:
CONDITION 1: STEADY GROWTH	favorable	positive
CONDITION 2: DECELERATED GROWTH	unfavorable	negative
CONDITION 3: FLAT LINE	unfavorable	negative
CONDITION 4: RATE CUT	unfavorable	negative
CONDITION 5: OMISSION	unfavorable	positive
CONDITION 6: ACCELERATION/RESTART	favorable	positive

Every investor has one of two postures with regard to any given stock (at least, putting aside the possibility of being short). The investor either (1) is already in the stock or (2) is out of but might be considering getting into it. For this reason, the six dividend signal conditions listed in the tables above have specific meanings for the two groups of investors, namely the "ins" and the "outs":

DIVIDEND TREND CONDITION	IF IN:	IF OUT:
CONDITION 1: STEADY GROWTH	Hold	Buy
CONDITION 2: DECELERATED GROWTH	Sell	Avoid
CONDITION 3: FLAT LINE	SELL!	Avoid
CONDITION 4: RATE CUT	—	Avoid
CONDITION 5: OMISSION	—	Buy(!)
CONDITION 6: ACCELERATION/RESTART	Hold	Buy

Investors following the above rules will see that they are internally logically consistent across the in/out border: what is a buy for the outsider is a hold for those already in the stock. What is a sell for the former owner is an avoid for the lucky outsider. Note the two blank sectors in the decision matrix: Conditions 4 and 5 produce no action signal for a holder of the stock because these conditions are almost universally preceded by Conditions 2 and/or 3, which were selling signals. If an investor is following the system faithfully, he or she would have sold the stock in a timely fashion under Condition 2 or certainly Condition 3 (whichever occurred first) and therefore would be among the "outs" before a Condition 4 or 5 occurs. For the sake of completeness, the reader might wish to pencil in "sell", perhaps in parentheses, in the blanks of the matrix, on the rare chance that these conditions might occur. Basically, however it is extremely unlikely that an investor actually following this system would ever be the owner of a stock when it moves into Condition 4 or 5.

Two exceptions are possible, and deserve mention. First, a major physical disaster (e.g., an earthquake or a nuclear accident) could befall a company which, immediately prior, had been in Condition 6 or 1. Such an external event is outside the purview of this book to predict; the signal system cannot fairly be held accountable for such aberrations. Second, on occasion a severely negative regulatory decision will be imposed on a company that until that time was growing comfortably and raising dividends regularly. In such a circumstance, it is possible for stage 2 and 3 to be bypassed and Condition 4 to follow Condition 1 directly.

In such relatively rare instances, the regulatory decision must be interpreted immediately as tantamount to a pre-announcement of Condition 4 or 5: while management will express disappointment or outrage over the "unfair and unjustified" treatment and will promise to pursue all available legal appeals, the die is cast and a pall will overhang the stock. Sell it! (It will be highly difficult, from a public relations perspective, for the board of directors and management simultaneously to continue increasing dividends as if nothing is wrong—while maintaining before the press, regulators, and the courts that the recent regulatory decision constitutes a financial disaster; the only credible course will be to move to Condition 3, 4, or 5—and the most convincing posture would be to move directly to Condition 4 or 5. That is precisely what the Consolidated Edison board did in April 1974: it omitted.)

The investor—trust me on this!—wants to be far off on the sidelines when the company's board faces the reality of needing to reduce or omit the dividend (Condition 4 or 5) for financial or political/credibility reasons. The dividend-signal system, if followed in the most disciplined and cautious manner, will save the investor emotional upset and risk to capital because a Condition 2 or 3 is viewed as a sufficiently strong warning to cause selling the stock and moving proceeds to other companies' stocks where Condition 1 is still in force.

SUMMARY

We have just revealed the executive summary of the utility dividend-signal system. In the following chapter we will review the dividend statuses in detail and indicate why—sometimes counter to what seems logical —each of the six dividend-trend conditions represents a buy, hold, sell, or avoid signal for investors.

The prior chapter developed a simple set of just six conditions for any utility stock. These are identified by trend and/or acceleration of the dividend rate as most recently declared by the Board of Directors. To review, the implied actions for investors, depending upon whether they currently own (are "in") the stock or not (are "out") are as follows:

	INVESTMENT ACTION	
DIVIDEND TREND CONDITION	IF IN:	IF OUT:
CONDITION 1: STEADY GROWTH	Hold	Buy
CONDITION 2: DECELERATED GROWTH	Sell	Avoid
CONDITION 3: FLAT LINE	SELL!	Avoid
CONDITION 4: RATE CUT	—	Avoid
CONDITION 5: OMISSION	—	Buy(!)
CONDITION 6: ACCELERATION/RESTART	Hold	Buy

The purpose of this chapter is to discuss the rationale for each of the above buy/hold/avoid/sell advices. Attention is given here to the news background and to the psychological aspects of the market condition at each phase in the cycle. Investors should remember that fundamentals (earnings and dividends, as discounted by interest rates) drive value in the long term. But even though investing in utilities is generally thought of as a dispassionate and conservative investment program, it is important to remember that investor psychology—swings between overoptimism (greed) and overpessimism (fear)—creates short-term price movements. While we attempt to keep a long-term perspective, we live from day to day in the environment of short-term swings in sentiment. If we succumb to the perspective of the short term we become its victim; if we keep the perspective and discipline to use short-term extremes of emotion about news to our advantage, we become successful contrarian investors—buying refrigerators in winter and selling our straw hats in the summer.

Let us discuss the news and psychological background of each of the conditions and see how it justifies the investment action signals assigned. Note, along the way, the consistency between the advices for the "ins" and the "outs:" what the "outs" should avoid the "ins" are advised to sell or have already sold on prior signals. When the "ins" are advised to hold or buy more, the "outs" are also advised to buy. This symmetry coincides with an important investment truth which should be used in any industry, not just utilities: since the decision to hold (and it should be a proactive choice, not a default from laziness or paralysis) is a decision to redeploy yesterday's capital again in the same security for today, it follows that one should hold only if one would actually be a buyer today. Any lesser degree of conviction means the holder is playing the greater-fool game by expecting other investors to buy and thereby support the price.

THE STATE OF CONTENTMENT: CONDITION 1

In earlier chapters the theme of investing for total return rather than for maximum current cash return has been stressed. We have established that a rising dividend indicates corporate health for the utility (unless it is created artificially via a rising payout ratio). In any period of steady interest rates, a rising dividend rate should drive a rising stock price. A dividend not being increased by the directors is a danger sign; the relatively high current yield it provides is, after being adjusted for the risk to principal, inferior to the combination of more moderate cash yield plus price appreciation driven by a rising dividend stream. Therefore, a dividend being periodically raised in conformity with established patterns of frequency and growth rate is the desirable, steady-state condition for utilities investors (see Table 15.1).

TABLE 15.1 Example of Insignificant Slip in Dividend Growth Rate				
YEAR	DIVIDEND RATES		INCREASE	PERCENT INCREASE
	OLD	NEW	(CONSTANT)	(SLIPPING)
1	$1.00	$1.04	$0.04	4.0%
2	$1.04	$1.08	$0.04	3.85%
3	$1.08	$1.12	$0.04	3.70%
4	$1.12	$1.16	$0.04	3.57%
5	$1.16	$1.20	$0.04	3.45%

Table 15.1 illustrates the mathematics of slight slippage in percentage growth rates; what defines the end of "constant" growth is any decrease in the amount of increase. For example, if the quarterly dividend rate has lately been raised by three cents, once a year, and is now raised by just two cents in the current period, this is a negative signal.

As long as the dividend is being raised at a constant rate, the present owner-investor should be content to hold (providing, of course, that macro indicators such as political events and the direction of inflation or officially set interest rates are not generating an overall "sell" signal for all yield-driven investments). This is the state of contentment, or Condition 1. An outsider considering purchase may do so. The final filter will be to check to assure that the payout ratio has not been increased for above prior norms. Condition 1 is thus a hold for the "ins" and a buy for the "outs." This will be a period of relative tranquillity in which interest-rate wiggles and normal daily or weekly price fluctuations cause minor moves in the stock price but should be ignored. The focus should remain on the dividend growth rate for any news-driven sign it might change, and certainly for any actual change by the directors.

CONDITION 2: A SUBTLE NEGATIVE SIGNAL NOT TO BE IGNORED

Condition 2 is a bit subtle, and arguably may seem not to exist in the case of small decreases in the percentage growth rate. (Many boards prefer not to declare dividends in tiny fractions of a cent per share, so rates declared may produce slight percentage-growth declines due merely to rounding as was just seen in Table 15.1).

A true Condition-2-type reduction in the dividend growth rate—one in which the *pennies-amount* of increase is smaller than in prior periods—does have meaning and must be honored with a sale action. There will be the temptation to reason that "they still declared an increase, which isn't really too bad a sign." Do not rationalize or be forgiving. The directors deliberately chose to reduce the amount of increase. They might have chosen to continue the past pattern, but they opted instead to change it to a less favorable one. Redeploy your money into other companies' shares where directors are not flashing this kind of negative signal.

Again, it will be important and profitable to remember the above-stated rule of thumb about doing what is *un*comfortable. The weight of evidence currently visible to you as an individual investor will seem to favor holding the stock despite the deliberate reduction in dividend growth rate. There will be comfort from such factors as the long uninterrupted history of dividend payments, the fact that there has been at least some increase in each of the past so many years, the fact that directors did declare at least a little increase, and so on. There may even be a logical explanation that seems to represent less than an imminent danger: regulatory uncertainty over a pending rate case is a bit higher than in the past; the company does need extra cash for a major plant expansion; environmental compliance costs are indeed a greater drag than in the past; the effective tax rate has risen due to changes in accounting rules or tax law.

There will be a temptation to be forgiving, to give the benefit of the doubt to the company (and therefore to the stock) pending further evidence. The problem is precisely that by the time the further evidence does come in for thousands of investors to see plainly, if the news is negative the stock will already be lower than now. You may feel most comfortable still holding the stock because nothing dramatically negative has occurred (yet), and you will feel at least vaguely uncomfortable or less than fully justified in selling it on such seemingly tiny negative evidence as a drop in the growth rate. But remember that you need to escape your comfort area when making investment decisions. Successful investing requires foresight into possible future scenarios, not reliance on the weight of past evidence. But all the foresight in the world is of no value if inertia or rationalization block action. If you are not prepared to act on signals by issuing a sell order when a signal is received, you might as well ignore all news about your investments. If that is your plan, please pass this book along to a friend so it can do someone a bit of good.

The would-be investor looking into a utility stock for possible purchase must be very careful to examine a full history of the dividend pattern. This is necessary to assure that an actual Condition 2 is not mistaken due to too-cursory an inspection for a Condition 1 stock (which can be bought). Table 15.2 indicates how this danger arises.

TABLE 15.2	Possible Erroneous Positive Interpretation of Latest Growth Rate		
			—— CONDITION ——
YEAR	GROWTH RATE	ACTUAL	FALSE CALL BY NEW OBSERVER
1	4%	1	
2	4%	1	
3	4%	1	
4	2.5%	2	
5	2.5%	2	1

If the year-5 dividend decision (+2.5%) is viewed only in the context of year 4, it appears benign. But a deeper look into history reveals that in context of years 1 through 3 the directors' latest action represents a confirmation of the caution flag sent up in year 4.

Whether the signal is new or older, the investor must remember not to rationalize. True, 2.5% is a better growth rate than zero. But it is a negative signal following the higher prior rate! Directors in year 4 knew or suspected something which may only become publicly evident (resulting in a much lower stock price) later on. The prudent investor will take the hint as soon as Condition 2 begins.

CONDITION 3: RED ALERT!

Condition 3, in which there is zero growth in the dividend rate, may appear to be acceptable to the naive. But in truth it is fraught with peril. There is the danger of taking comfort from past history—the company may have paid dividends for decades and the investor may not understand that such history is irrelevant to present circumstances. Another major source of danger is the temptation of chasing high current yield, discussed in some detail in Chapters 11 and 12. Not only is the yield-seeking investor at risk of falling into the high-yield trap, there is danger from brokerage advice as well.

If a broker is ignorant of the truth (or—yes, Virginia—is greedy and unscrupulous enough to ignore it), that broker knows that selling high yield to clients is easier work than selling less-than-high yield. So investors are likely to be shown numerous high-yield "opportunities" in utility stocks. These should be politely but firmly declined. Remember that risk and reward run parallel in the investment world: you may not know the details of the danger, but the market is signalling its presence by providing a high yield out of line with other stocks in the same industry.

Many naive investors are tempted to reach for 1% or 2% higher current cash yield in a utility stock rather than play the safer game of lower current yield plus growth (i.e., total return). What such investors are ignoring is that the consequences of a wrong bet are devastating. A dividend cut or omission, which often follows a Condition 3 alert, might easily rob the stockholder of 25% of invested capital or more. That's 12 to 25 years' worth of extra yield. Unless the investor can say with assurance that the odds of a cut or omission are less than 1:25, the high-yield bet is not worth taking. By flattening the growth rate to zero, directors have in effect already said that the odds of big, bad news are real.

Conclusion: the "outs" should definitely stay out (avoid) and the "ins" should get out (sell) if they did not already do so in Condition 2. With well over 100 other utilities to consider, why sit on the hot seat of a Condition 3?

CONDITION 4: A LIGHTNING STRIKE FOLLOWED BY LINGERING CLOUDS

When a utility's dividend is reduced (Condition 4) it is a sign of major distress. Except in unusual circumstances (described in the prior chapter), earlier signals such as deceleration or zero dividend growth will have typically preceded the reduction. The "outs" will have avoided the stock already. There should be, under the signal system developed in this book, no "ins." The naive and those paralyzed by inertia or afraid to take even a small loss will remain as holders. Those in the know, now including the reader, will have taken shelter before the storm's full fury hits. Dr. Edmund Bergler, in his excellent volume *The Psychology of Gambling*, quotes Tallyrand's response to the question "how would you act in such a situation?" He said, "Very simple. I would never get *into* such a situation."

Once a utility's board of directors has taken the distasteful step of reducing the dividend, the stock can be consigned to the dormant category. Why? Those who held on too long (ignoring Conditions 2 or 3) and then exited after the bad news (Condition 4) will be unhappy with the stock and will be loathe to return after being burned once. Cautious investors, whether individuals or institutional managers, will prudently wait for a possible "other shoe" to drop. They will be thinking: "What will the next change be—a further cut, an omission, or no growth from this low level?"

None of those scenarios is inviting to prospective buyers, so the stock will lose sponsorship. The only satisfactory cure for the dormancy induced by a dividend cut is a subsequent increase, even if a small one. Visualize this situation: you are a potential buyer of a utility stock whose directors' most recent dividend change was a cut from $2.00 to $1.00 per year. The prudent course is to wait for some positive signal. Ask these questions:

- Can't they even be confident enough to inch that rate back up to $1.04—anything to say the last signal (a 50% cut!) is no longer the primary indication of how things look?

- If they are not confident enough to give some positive indication, who am I to outguess them as to whether they will raise the dividend next or cut it further?

This kind of thinking, plus the bad taste of earlier losses, will dominate investors' reasoning as long as the stock stays in Condition 4. Sensible investors have no reason to be anywhere but out until the clouds of uncertainty are lifted.

The three ways for directors to resolve the uncertainty are by re-starting dividend growth (a subcategory of Condition 6), by cutting further (not really a resolution since the stock remains in Condition 4 but most likely at an even lower price), and by omitting the dividend altogether (Condition 5). Here is where the greatest surprise occurs for investors.

CONDITION 5: THE IRONY OF IRONIES

The two signals that most investors most frequently doubt and can least frequently bring themselves to honor are Conditions 2 and 5. Condition 2 is by far the more subtle. Typically, however, the most difficult rule of the six to follow—particularly because utilities investors are by nature risk averse—is the buy signal provided by Condition 5. Yes, a dividend omission is a signal to buy the utility's stock! Imagine the broker calling up a client and saying, "I've got terrible news: Amalgamated Central Power and Gas just omitted its dividend, so I think you ought to jump in and buy 500 shares right now." You have probably never had such a call from a broker, nor should you anticipate receiving one—unless your broker has read this book and knows his or her market history unusually well! Brokers are every bit as much the victims of human nature as are individual investors.

We all find it very difficult to do what makes us feel uncomfortable. And yet this departure from the personal comfort zone is the linchpin of the equation for successful investment results. What makes the investor (and the broker, and even the professional money manager) feel most comfortable and confident of correctness is what is already well "known" in terms of publicly disseminated and generally understood news and opinion. But by definition that set of facts and opinions is what investors collectively *have already acted upon*. Therefore, what makes the investor comfortable as a basis for decisions in what is already "in the market" or "in the price." Only contradictory future information or opinions, for better or for worse, will influence the price to move from its present level. And, by its nature, such differing information will be discomforting to those who thought they already had the situation figured out.

Placing a buy order under Condition 5 will never feel comfortable. The weight of current evidence, namely the stark fact that directors just did the nearly unthinkable by omitting the dividend, will be shouting, "be careful, there's trouble here!" The market, which is to say the collective current opinions of thousands of other investors, will be confirming the nonholder's worst suspicions: the stock price will be dropping like a rock. Trust officers will be forced (using their 20/20 hindsight) to sell the stock because it produces no current income; mutual fund portfolio managers may labor under similar requirements and at the least will not want to show the stock among current holdings at the end of the next reporting period. Individual investors by the thousands either will panic due to the price drop or will sell the stock to seek income-producing alternatives, or both. All those around you will be rushing to sell.

This rush of the lemmings represents a classic opportunity to buy, as was the case during the worldwide stock market crash on October 19, 1987. But buying will not be a comfortable move to make. With the context of the preceding paragraphs as your guide, however, you now understand that what is best for your investment success will be what makes you feel least comfortable, not most comfortable.

Short of bankruptcy, the worst possible news for an income investor is a dividend omission. It suspends the income stream for an unpredictable period and reduces the value of the asset. It causes severe emotional pain. It often leads to self reproach: "I should have sold sooner, when they stopped raising the rate," for example. For reasons cited above, the dividend omission causes a selling panic in the stock, and panics usually define a price bottom. In this blackest of current-news environments, it is obvious to all observers just how bad the company's condition has become. Contrarians, awake! What "everyone" already knows is now in the price of the stock. The news, and the stock price, can only get better from this point.

What, if anything, can go wrong to make things even worse? Could the company go out of business altogether? Not if the city or state wants electric power or phone service. Could there be no payment to owners for the assets if a public authority takes over? Not in any legal/investment scenario you want to face in the United States! Could the dividend stay at zero for several years? Possibly. Could the company go into Chapter 11, prolonging the agony? Yes: Public Service of New Hampshire, Columbia Gas System, and El Paso Electric did, in the recent era. But as bad as the PNH case was, its stock doubled after the omission and before the further troubles that eventually drove the Chapter 11 filing.

It will be very uncomfortable to do, but when Condition 5 occurs the "outs" should become "ins." The only excuse for delaying beyond a few weeks past the shock wave is the nearby onset of tax-loss selling season. Buy into that pressure in December, in that case. For reasons Tallyrand explained, there are no "ins" among my readers when Condition 5 first occurs.

CONDITION 6: THE EXHILARATION OF HEALING

Condition 6, the acceleration of the dividend stream's growth rate, is possible in any of five contexts. A partial re-instatement of cash dividends following an omission is, mathematically, a Condition 6 event, so it represents a buy signal. Very cautious investors will have been too risk averse to dare entering at Condition 5. They will insist on waiting for the "all clear" signal that they hear when directors do start declaring dividends again. But a restart is never a total news surprise: conditions at the company have been healing for some time, and investors have been asking "when" rather than "whether" lately. The stock has been creeping ahead as late Condition-5 buyers enter and as more and more of the long-time holders who did not panic on the omission regain hope of eventual full recovery and hold on as the price gradually improves. When Condition 6 comes after an omission, the stock is a buy, but a late buy compared with the opportunity at time of the omission. The reason, again, is that "everyone" already can see the good news by the time some level of the dividend is restarted.

Other kinds of accelerations are probably more key events. A re-acceleration after a Condition 2 (deceleration) or especially after Condition 3 (zero growth) or Condition 4 (a cut) is really good news. A Condition 6 after a 3 or 4 is especially important in that it finally removes the dark clouds that have been overhead since those signals were given. In such cases Condition 6 is a buy signal for the "outs." Occasionally a company will move from steady growth (Condition 1) to acceleration. This is a pleasant surprise and signals firmly that buying (for the "outs") or further accumulations (for the "ins") remain appropriate.

Investors must be aware that an occasional Condition 6 can sometimes lead to a later false reading of Condition 2. Here is how this happens: suppose a company has been increasing the dividend at about 4% per annum for a while (years 1 through 4 in Table 15.3) while earnings have actually been growing a bit faster. So the payout ratio has been sliding to a bit below what the directors feel is desirable or appropriate. Directors may for one or two years (years 5 and 6) accelerate the rate to adjust the payout ratio. Once that process is completed, a return to 5% or 4% growth (year 7 below) reflects a return to steady state rather than a Condition-2 deceleration.

TABLE 15.3 Possible Erroneous Positive Interpretation
of Latest Growth Rate

| | | —— CONDITION —— | |
YEAR	GROWTH RATE	ACTUAL	FALSE CALL BY NEW OBSERVER
1	4%	1	
2	4%	1	
3	4%	1	
4	4%	2	
5	6%	6	
6	6%	1	
7	5% or 4%	1 (as vs. year 4)	2

Thus all six conditions are explained, in terms of company fundamentals as well as investor psychology. The most ironic and contrarian signal is 5 (omission). The most alarming signal is 3 (zero growth), for it hints of even worse news to follow. The most subtle is 2, but it should be heeded, for it is often a harbinger of ill fortune, even if an early one. The most important context for investors to maintain is an orientation to what might come next that is different, not what has already become known. For the risk-averse investor, change that is negative is what is most to be sniffed out early. Better to pay a brokerage commission now than to lose considerably more in capital —or in rising income—later on!

Pictures Worth a Thousand Words

This chapter provides the reader with a pictorial history of how utility stocks have acted under various dividend conditions during the past 10 years or longer. The graphs are used with the kind permission of Long Term Values, a highly useful reference service available from William O'Neil & Company in Los Angeles (see Appendix II for details). Another useful reference tool is *The SRC Blue Book*, published by Securities Research Corp. in Boston. Its key virtue is charts plotted on logarithmic scales so the dividend growth rates are readily apparent. However, its coverage list is not as complete.

CONDITION 1: STEADY GROWTH

TECO Energy, serving the Tampa area, is an excellent example of a company with regular dividend increases at roughly a constant percentage rate. The timing and frequency of the increases can be seen by noting the small upward-pointing arrows under the "D" initials (standing for dividend rate) across the top of the graph. The approximate shape of the price pattern of TECO (see Figure 16.1) can be used as a standard for comparing other companies' chart histories.

Figure 16.1   TECO Energy, Inc.

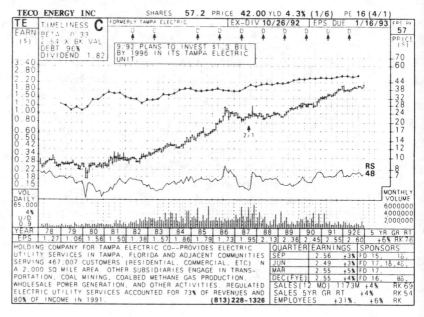

Another company with almost as strong a pattern, one still classified as Condition 1, is SCEcorp, serving a large area in California. Dividend increases in recent years have been made in equal cents' increments, so the percentage growth rate is slowing somewhat. Until a smaller-cents increase is declared, continue to classify SCE as showing "steady growth" (see Figure 16.2).

Figure 16.2 SCEcorp

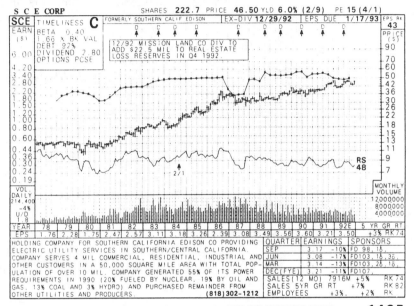

UTILITY-ELECTRIC POWER   149E

CONDITION 2: DECELERATING GROWTH

Several companies, at various times, illustrate deceleration of dividend growth, because either the frequency or size of increases was slowing. First, examine Delmarva Power & Light, a mid-Atlantic company. In 1985 it became a Condition 2 situation, the first sign of time to step aside. The company's classification shifted to the more dangerous Condition 3 in 1989 when it failed to continue increasing its dividend rate. Note the subsequent underperformance in price (see Figure 16.3).

Figure 16.3 Delmarva Power and Light

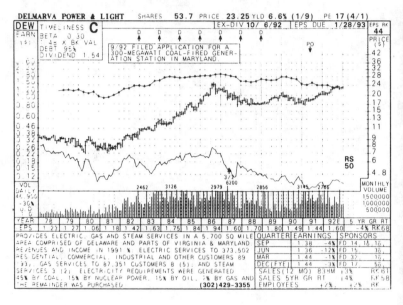

Another electric company which decelerated its dividend growth is Boston Edison. This was evident in 1986-1988 when its increases became less frequent. The stock topped out in 1986-1987. By mid-1989, it was clear that BSE had moved to Condition 3, by failing twice in two years to raise its rate. In December 1989 the company cut its rate moderately (then Condition 4). In a rather unusual sequence, just one year later it began a series of accelerating increases, so it remained classified in Condition 6 as of early 1993 (see Figure 16.4).

Figure 16.4 Boston Edison Co.

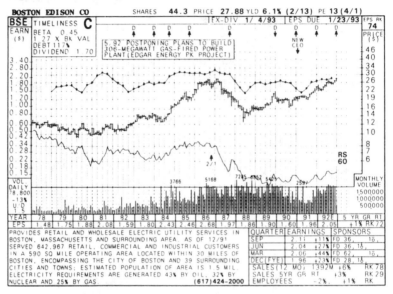

Idaho Power provides an unusually varied group of signals over the past decade. It had been in Condition 1, with steady increases, through 1985. Its 1986 increase was only $0.08 per share, representing a 20% slowdown, so at that point the stock fell into Condition 2 of decelerating growth. Note that the price crested in 1986. In 1987 and 1988 the company moved into Condition 3 by failing to declare any increase. The renewed increase in 1990 seemed to put the company in the accelerating Condition 6 group— but only briefly. Dividends were not increased in 1991-1992, placing IDA back in Condition 3, meaning no growth. In a period of falling interest rates, the stock again underperformed by doing no better than moving basically sideways (see Figure 16.5).

Figure 16.5 Idaho Power

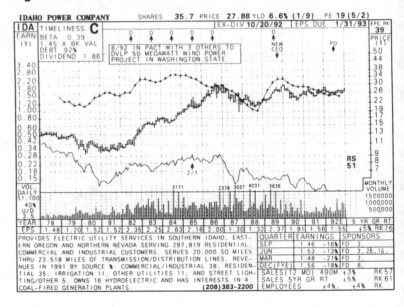

CONDITION 3: PRIOR GROWTH, NOW ZERO GROWTH

A very current illustration of a move into Condition 3, meaning zero growth after prior growth, is provided by Cincinnati Bell. In early 1991, CSN stopped raising its rate, moving it into Condition 3 status. Note how the stock has dropped virtually in half since its 1989 highs (made when telephone stocks in general had run up too fast). Contrast CSN's price action (see Figure 16.6) and total return with that of GTE Corp., whose chart is shown later in this chapter.

Figure 16.6 Cincinnati Bell, Inc.

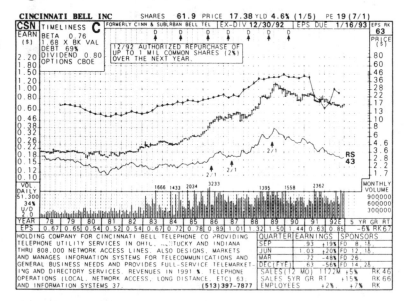

ENSERCH Corp. illustrates how a utility stock's zero-growth dividend signal can be followed by the more disastrous sequel, a dividend cut. In 1982 ENSERCH moved from steady growth to zero growth, putting it into Condition 3 for about the next four years. Although the chart fails to include a downward arrow, in fact ENSERCH cut its rate in half to $0.80 in mid-1986. Through late 1992, there had been no further change. But the first quarter of 1993 brought another cut of 75% to $0.20 per year, so ENS remains in Condition 4. Investors have punished the stock for a decade, dropping its price nearly in half while interest rates have fallen significantly (see Figure 16.7).

Figure 16.7   ENSERCH Corp.

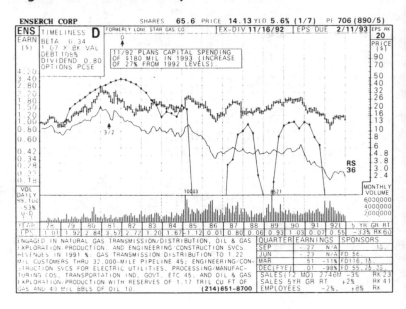

CONDITION 4: REDUCTION

A similar fate recently befell shareholders of Chicago-based Commonwealth Edison. By failing to increase its dividend any further in 1983, the company fell into what became a prolonged Condition 3. In September 1992 the other shoe dropped when directors cut the annual rate from $3.00 to $1.60. Now CWE is in Condition 4 (see Figure 16.8).

Figure 16.8 Commonwealth Edison

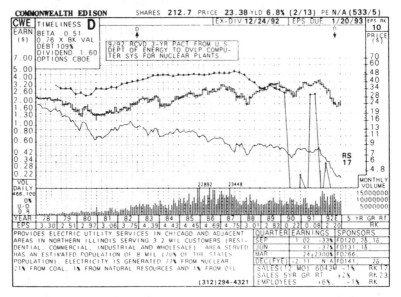

Pinnacle West Capital (formerly Arizona Public Service) followed four years of flat dividends starting in 1984, with a dividend cut in 1988. At that point, having failed to rally following the 1987 crash, the stock was in Condition 4. The final blow came in late 1989, with an omission (Condition 5). Note that, despite talk of bankruptcy and the constant glare of publicity surrounding the bank bailout provided to the MeraBank subsidiary, the omission marked a panic bottom and the stock approximately tripled in the next 36 months. But further price damage had first occurred during the Condition 4 period, illustrating that such a situation can be resolved only by renewed growth or an omission (see Figure 16.9).

Figure 16.9 Pinnacle West Capital

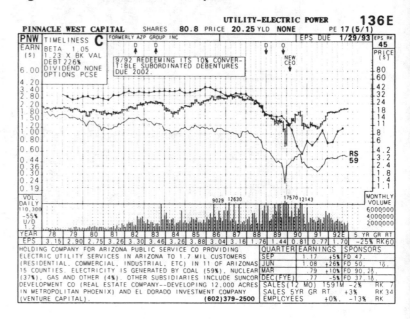

An early-1984 reduction (Condition 4) was followed by a partial restorative increase (Condition 6) at Connecticut-based United Illuminating in 1985. But no further increases were forthcoming for some time (reversion to Condition 3) as the company faced uncertainty over its stake in the Seabrook plant in New Hampshire. More recently, Condition 6 has been restored with two consecutive annual $0.12 rate increases. This was a happier resolution and the stock in early 1993 was trading at all-time highs (see Figure 16.10).

Figure 16.10   United Illuminating Co.

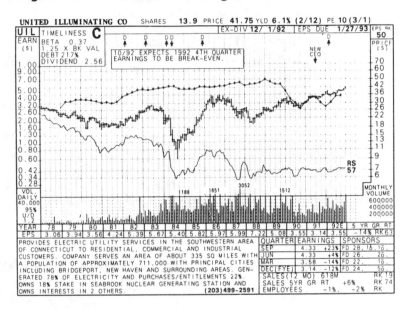

CONDITION 5: OMISSION

One of the most spectacular omissions was that of General Public Utilities, whose subsidiary operates Three Mile Island. The company omitted its dividend in 1979 (Condition 5) and the stock bottomed almost immediately despite the cloud of nuclear worries beamed to investors on the evening news long thereafter. In the ensuing fourteen years, the stock has multiplied its owners' value 12-fold. Omissions truly are amazing and surprising buy signals! Dividends were not resumed until 1988 but have grown rapidly since, giving the stock a Condition 6 rating at publication time (see Figure 16.11).

Figure 16.11 General Public Utilities

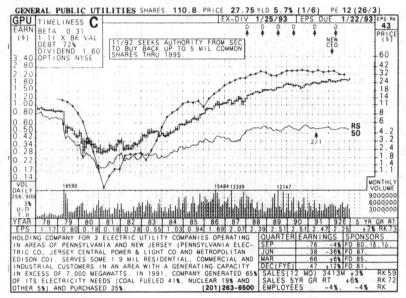

Regulatory woes prompted two dividend cuts (Condition 4) *and* an omission by directors of Michigan-based CMS Energy (then Consumers Power) all in 1984—a busy year. Once Condition 5 finally prevailed with the omission, the stock promptly hit bottom. After a spectacular percentage rise, and a resumption (Condition 6 in late 1990), the stock has again faltered as no further increases have been declared, marking a reversion to Condition 3. Its early-1993 price was down about 50%— without a dividend cut! This clearly illustrates the urgency of selling on a Condition 3 signal (see Figure 16.12).

Figure 16.12 CMS Energy Corp

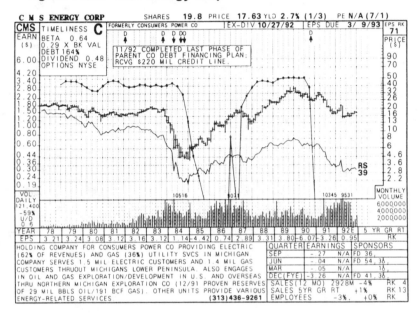

CONDITION 6: RESUMPTION OR ACCELERATION

Another company which suffered through first a flat-dividend period and then a cut is ONEOK (pronounced One-O.K.). This Oklahoma-based gas pipeline began raising its rate again (Condition 1) in 1988 and then accelerated its dividend growth to about 8% in 1991, earning itself a Condition 6 rating at press time. Note the long-delayed price improvement that began in early 1991 with the change in status (see Figure 16.13).

Figure 16.13   ONEOK, Inc.

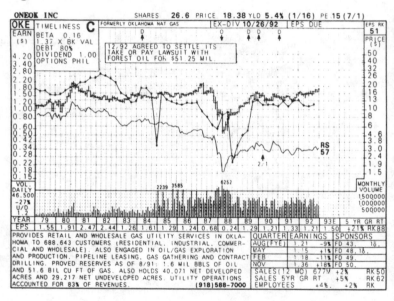

A highly positive signal in the form of dividend acceleration has been given by directors of GTE Corp. (formerly General Telephone & Electronics). The dividend (adjusted for a subsequent 3:2 split) had been rising by about $0.05 per year until an eight-cent jump in 1987. Following a 2:1 split in 1990, further rapid increases have been declared. These accelerations have earned GTE a Condition 6 ranking. As of early 1993 the dividend rate had been raised to $1.82, up over 30% from just $1.37 as recently as 1989. The stock price has outrun those of nearly all other phone companies in response. And yet at early 1993 it yielded a solid 5.3% and was showing growth in the range of 6% to 7% (see Figure 16.14).

Figure 16.14 GTE Corp.

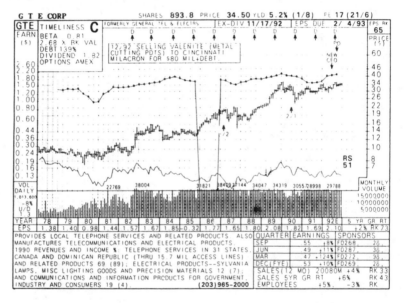

This chapter has provided visual examples of the strong influence that dividend growth signals have on stock price. While the utility investor is interested in income, the more important measure of success is total return. A high dividend accompanied by a stagnant or falling stock price is no bargain. The charts chosen for illustrative purposes show that Condition 5 (omission) and Condition 6 (acceleration) are the most powerful triggers of price growth. And a steady increase (Condition 1) provides continuing official reassurance, assisting price appreciation.

SEVENTEEN

News travels fast. Especially in our electronic age. And particularly if it happens to be bad news.

The dividend-signal system described and illustrated in Chapters 14-16 should help now-informed utilities investors to avoid almost any exposure to dividend cuts or omissions. Dividend-growth trends are the most critical news items for you. But other sometimes-negative news deserves specific attention and mental preparation as well.

In this chapter we explore patterns in stocks when bad news occurs, and specifically when the news is unexpected or highly disturbing. This material is intended as background for occasions when misfortune strikes, as inevitably it will. It should help you to (1) be braced for what price reaction is likely and (2) make intelligent tactical decisions on what to do: whether to grit your teeth and take the harsh rain in your face, or whether to turn and run for shelter. Too often, investors give in to the swings of emotion in the market—selling out when news is bad, only to find later that they were part of the selling-panic bottom. This chapter seeks to aid the reader in dealing with bad situations as well (i.e., as rationally) as possible.

Some qualifying points are in order. First, the following discussion *relates only to company-specific news events,* not to trends in the general market as measured by the "averages." Second, it concerns sharp price declines driven by negative news, and not routine price declines that are merely technical corrections. Third, the discussion below excludes acquisition stocks, where the

151

ongoing sequence of news is highly unpredictable and where events and emotions are dramatic. Fourth, situations driven by continuous (non-discrete) outside influences are also excluded. These would include ongoing interest-rate trends, secular increases in oil prices, and pending environmental legislation—stories that have lives of their own and so are not discrete, one-day news items. Finally, the context is a sideways or higher market environment: reactions are worse in total but sometimes initially less severe during bear markets.

Our subject is the phenomenon of material, unexpected, discrete, bad news for a company — an earthquake or major hurricane fit the criteria. Both materiality and surprise are important, for lack of these will not move a stock price much. Discreteness of the news is important conceptually, because it greatly affects the timing and extent of price reactions. Discrete news developments, in the context of this discussion, are one-time items (or at least so they can reasonably seem for at least a while) that do not breed suspicion of further negatives to come.

Sometimes an apparently discrete negative item (a director resigns) is followed by another piece of bad news (the company adopts more liberal accounting rules). In such a situation the clock starts running again in terms of counting days of market-price reaction. And quite often in such cases the newly-emerging pattern of clustered bad news means the stock will act like a non-discrete piece of bad news has occurred, since suspicions of deeper trouble have been kindled.

The following are examples of material, unexpected, discrete bad news (let's call these MUD items for short):

- For a telephone or an electric company, a major storm that causes service disruptions and repair expense well beyond normal bounds

- For a gas distribution company, damage clearly caused by an outside force such as an earthquake or by a fire or explosion in a nearby plant—a case where no fault is likely to be laid to the company

- For any type of utility, a disappointing rate decision not resulting in a cautionary management statement about future dividend policy

- A one-quarter earnings surprise caused by nonrecurring factors such as a supplier's strike or storm damage, or by write-offs that are not part of an established company or industry pattern

- An announcement that the company is exiting from its single non-utility business, accompanied by a write-down.

By contrast, here are some nondiscrete negative events:

- Delayed, impaired, or canceled inclusion of construction into the rate base (many nuclear electrics have foundered on this one!)

- A new law or court ruling that creates broader concepts of liability whose true costs cannot be calculated presently

- Well-documented environmental/medical evidence linking the company's product with disease (water companies with mercury poisoning and nuclear generators' radiation, for example)

- A developing pattern of adverse local regulatory treatment (this usually leads later to flat or reduced dividends!)

- A major workplace or ecological accident in which the company clearly will be or probably will be found at least partly at fault—or one whose investigation will linger on in news coverage

- The unexplained resignation of a very senior executive or financial officer with any hint of mystery or scandal

- Announcement of a decline in earnings (or the expectation of such) for reasons that reflect management weaknesses (poor control) or lack of reasonable foresight

- Government probes of the company for possible antitrust violations, false documentation, ineffective expense control, etc.

- S.E.C. investigation into possible securities violations on the part of the company or one or more officers

- Disclosure that one or more past financial statements were inaccurate and that it will take some time to investigate before issuing revised reports

- Indications that a series of write-offs may follow

- Any other news announcement which, while appearing to be discrete, represents a contradiction of previous management representations to analysts or the press

The key difference between the two lists of examples is the apparent degree of closure versus open-endedness. An old market cliché holds that the market can handle good news, and can even handle bad news, but uncertainty drives it crazy. The difference between finite, known, bad news and uncertain but bad-portent news is reflected in the way investors react.

There are parallels in everyday life: when we visit the doctor we want the diagnosis now; the waiting and imagining are deadly on the mental state. Or, at work, when there are rumors of layoffs or salary cuts, we want to know our own fate now rather than suffer through the uncertainty. The market's reaction to open-ended bad-implications news is more drawn out, since an uneasy feeling creates less-severe selling pressure at first but leaves a dark cloud lingering long afterward. When the bad news is discrete, the reaction can be sharp but usually is relatively brief.

MUD bad news typically imposes a two-day or three-day negative price effect on the stock. In effect, it is a private emotional "crash," isolating one stock. The reasons for this pattern of typical duration have to do with news dissemination and absorption. The sharpness of the price reaction has almost certainly been compounded in recent years by the twin demons of short investment horizons and high concentration of institutional holdings.

When news is announced, it typically has a two-day life in the media, unless it is so major that prolonged follow-up coverage ensues. (Examples of the latter were Three Mile Island in the utilities area, the Bhopal chemical disaster and the Exxon Valdez accident, and in early 1992 the Dow-Corning breast-implant controversy.) On the day of a MUD bad-news announcement, unless the company arranges to have it released after the market closes, the item runs on the wire services and perhaps on the TV stock-market shows during the session. Some investors and traders react immediately. Then, the next day, the story—perhaps in greater length and detail—runs in the newspapers. More people now learn what happened (if they did not see or hear it on the evening TV or radio news), and they in turn can react.

Thus, for any meaningful negative news, one should generally expect a two-day price reaction at a minimum. But if the bad news occurs on a Thursday or Friday, a three-day reaction is very likely. This is because "weekend investors" react on reading the stock quotations in the Saturday and Sunday papers. Monday, they call their brokers and ask what caused the big drop the prior week; often they create a minor third wave of selling pressure. In cases where big bad news occurs on Friday, the three-day pattern can come into play if the general market happens to take a serious dive on Monday. There often follows a Tuesday-morning general rout, and that will let further air out of any stock that has just suffered bad publicity.

Two or three days' MUD bad news should be about the extent of the immediate damage. There will usually follow a period—perhaps two days to a week or longer—in which the stock at least steadies and sometimes tries to rally. Then, usually, one will observe a renewed price decline, but this one is usually much smaller than the first. The second decline occurs, typically, because the stock has run out of gas from bargain hunters attracted by the first crack, or because the technical chart pattern looks weak (not often a very important factor with utility shares), or because the general market weakens and this particular stock cannot hold in the face of a widespread decline.

It is important to anticipate how a stock will act on bad news so you can be deliberate in your response. The main points are (1) to distinguish carefully between discrete bad news and non-discrete bad news—which have very different longer-term implications for the hold/sell decision, and (2) to provide a set of expectations as to what kind of decline and following price stabilization can be realistically expected. The latter will help the unfortunate investor when the feeling of falling into a bottomless pit occurs. It will be useful to know that, while the price will probably not recover soon to its pre-news level, it will shortly stop declining and will provide at least a couple of days of stability and even bounce in which a better sale can usually be executed. If—due to inattention, lack of broker service, indecision, or denial—you have not sold the stock on the first day of bad news, you will know that by the third day's arrival it is already too late, and you should be pretty confident that holding for now will provide a modestly better sale opportunity in the several days following.

Many factors besides elapsed time can affect the price reaction. The following lead to steeper declines:

- Large institutional holdings (implying volume sales)

- Bad news occurring shortly before the end of a calendar quarter (institutional window dressers will want not to show a holding in quarterly portfolio lists)

- Lengthy past period of rising EPS and dividends (implying that the shock of bad news will be harsh)

- Stock having recently performed strongly rather than sideways or lower (implying a scramble to lock down profits)

- Coincidence of a sharply weaker market at just the same time company-specific news hits the stock itself (bargain hunters standing aside)

- Bad news smacking of a currently sensitive subject such as insider trading, ecological problems, health scare, or other hot-news type (these will engender a greater reaction by the public than will non-hot types of bad news).

Earlier mention was made of the occasional situation where a seemingly discrete bad-news item is followed by a second item. In this case, either the clock starts running again for two or three days, or the situation must be considered as an erosion problem where investors see the company's announcement as no longer discrete. A good example of this occurred in October 1989.

Phoenix-based Pinnacle West Capital, the parent company of both MeraBank and Arizona Public Service, announced a dividend omission late one afternoon. PNW stock moved fractionally lower to the close and broke sharply the next day.

The second full day of post-news trading brought a further drop, on lower volume. Normally, one would then have expected a stabilization and perhaps a bit of a snap-back rally. But then a major news wire interviewed a company spokesperson, who mentioned the theoretical possibility of a Chapter 11 bankruptcy filing to rid Pinnacle West of its troubled thrift unit. This second piece of bad news lengthened the period of sharp price drop for another two days. It was arrested only when an 80-point morning smash in the Dow Jones Industrials reversed to a four-point drop by the close. For anyone not already quite familiar with the Pinnacle West story, the mention of Chapter 11 created a new cloud of ongoing uncertainty. Thus the stock was no longer in the discrete bad news category. Subsequently the news continued to worsen until the bank was divested early in the period of expanding RTC losses.

This chapter has contrasted stock-specific, discrete bad news with new information that is open-ended in its implications and thus represents part of a pattern of deterioration. Without hesitation or denial or rationalized hope, one should sell a stock where the odor is one of gradual rot. More often than not, the nose knows the truth.

Having learned the dividend-signal system provided in the prior chapters, you will be attuned to a particular type of bad news the general public may not see at all or may pay scant heed. That is the disappointing dividend declaration. Such an action by the board of directors may cause little or no immediate price reaction. You, however, should not be lulled into complacency. Rather, seek a tactically advantageous exit point over the short term—usually if possible before the ex-dividend date. While the decelerated dividend need not prompt an instant, at-market sell order, it is a strong signal you ignore at your peril. You should take deliberate action quite shortly, even though not on the first day. You may be early in your exit, but this will prove better than being late when thousands of other investors have finally decided there is trouble enough to prompt their selling out.

The flip side of bad news for the holder is the potential opportunity it creates for the buyer-in-waiting. External events such as storms can provide good bargain-level entry points. The buyer must evaluate whether serious long-term damage to the dividend-growth rate is implied by the bad news. If the answer is no, and if the dividend signal is right, the bad news of the day can provide a good purchase level that may not last for long.

EIGHTEEN

Riding Interest-Rate Cycles for Maximum Gains

Much of this book has focused attention on the issue of selecting —and de-selecting—individual utility stocks. The central theme has been that the critical timing and selection variable is the stock's changing dividend growth rates. In effect, this approach represents an attempt to "beat the market" (in the sense of outperforming the averages) by selecting superior companies and weeding out those whose shares are likely to underperform. Since, at the very least, avoiding the loss of money is important to achieving investment success, stock selection is undeniably important. Without it, the investor may expect to achieve no better than average results—and many unsophisticated utility investors will usually do worse than that because of the capital-destroying trap of buying high-yield stocks. This chapter, by contrast, shifts attention from the specific to the general. Another highly important aspect of investing in utility stocks is the interest-rate cycle.

Interest, from the borrower's viewpoint, is the price or rate of rent paid to use another's money. From the lender's viewpoint, it is the price or rate of rent demanded and received from another who uses one's money. Economists speak of the rent on money as being the price demanded for forgoing consumption in favor of investment or saving. Like the price of oil or gold or tomatoes, the price of money fluctuates according to the supply of and demand for it. During a full economic cycle, interest rates will usually show very significant changes. (For example, a change from 8% to 10% and back is not 2% each way but a 25% rise and a 20% fall.)

Such changes can work to the advantage or the disadvantage of investors—and this is especially true for investors who focus their resources directly on securities oriented to producing income. Savers, people who leave their funds in the bank, choose to avoid and ignore the potential effects on capital driven by changes in interest rates. But by investing in bonds or utility shares you expose yourself to these changes. Therefore you need to understand them, be prepared for them, and be willing to act when appropriate. Such action can preserve capital against erosion as well as enhance it when rates move in your favor. Both kinds of gains are important. A loss avoided is every bit a profit achieved.

Three major factors, to be reviewed briefly below, influence the level and trend of interest rates:

- Changes and expected changes in price levels
- The pace and momentum of business activity
- Government policy regarding credit

Interest rates tend to reflect expectations about the changing level of prices. If prices of goods and services are expected to rise significantly, rational investors will demand a high rate of interest to compensate for the loss of purchasing power they expect while the money is in the hands of the borrower. It makes no sense for a money owner to lend a dollar for a year at less than 100% interest if it can be reasonably expected that it will take two dollars to buy a loaf of bread, now priced at one dollar, a year hence. Economic forecasts are usually less than fully accurate, so in practice the actual rate of price increase seldom precisely equals the predicted change. So the nominal interest rate agreed to may have only approximated the change in prices. The real interest rate is the nominal rate less the loss of purchasing power, and sometimes the real rate will prove to have been negative. Interest rates tend to be what economists call "sticky": they do not move as quickly as one might expect. At least part of this is due to the way people set their expectations for rates of price inflation, which is by roughly extrapolating recent experience. We tend to forecast "more of the same."

Another major factor driving interest rates to change over time is the pace and the changing momentum of business activity. Both business managers and consumers increase their purchasing activity as the economy becomes stronger. A great deal of spending, especially on big-ticket items, is done with borrowed money. More demand for money, such as occurs in a period of expansion, raises the rental rate or price of money, which we call the interest rate. In times of contraction and caution, demand for loans shrinks. As an inducement to potential borrowers, banks offer "bargain" loan rates. This phenomenon was quite visible in 1991 and 1992 as consumers pulled back and banks responded by cutting interest rates on loans.

The third factor driving changes in interest rates is government policy. This is the clearest of the three and therefore the easiest for investors to use as an action signal. The Federal Reserve System can influence interest rates in two ways (aside from day-to-day open-market operations). The Fed can change reserve requirements, which directly increases or decreases banks' legal authority to lend money. Banks respond to such tightening in part by rationing the available credit through higher interest rates. The Fed can also signal its preference as to the direction of interest rates by changing the discount rate. This is the rate of interest at which the Fed will lend money to banks. The discount rate sets the basic tone for the overall direction of all other interest rates and is considered a highly important signal. Investors will probably learn about changes in the discount rate in the newspapers or on radio or TV news. It is hardly an imposition to ask your stockbroker to keep you informed when such changes are made. This is a good way to assure that you do not miss an important signal.

In recent decades the Federal Reserve Board has been faced with the challenging task of balancing the control of price inflation against the accommodation of economic growth. Reducing the tradeoff to popular terms, the Board is said to choose between "fighting inflation" and "fighting recession." The Fed fights inflation by tightening credit availability and raising interest rates. It fights recession or promotes economic expansion by moving in the opposite direction. Investors in bonds and in utility stocks want to see interest rates move lower so that the market values of their income-producing securities will rise rather than fall. Therefore, a slack economy is good for utility stocks, while a strong economy accompanied by rising interest rates is bad for utility stocks.

The question utilities investors face is whether they should merely try to select superior individual stocks or whether, in addition, they should try to move into and out of the market to take advantage of changes in interest rates. Since interest rates change fairly significantly, the answer is that moving in and out of the market is more desirable than standing pat—even if you own only "good" stocks. This offends the sensibilities of investors who view themselves as conservative and oriented to the long term. But "the numbers" overwhelmingly support playing interest-rate cycles rather than ignoring them.

The fundamental reason is the equation for a stock price:

$$\text{Stock price} = \frac{\text{Dividend rate}}{\text{Required rate of cash return}}$$

The principal reason interest-rate changes cannot be dismissed is that changes in interest rates are larger than changes in dividend rates over the short term. Assuming a constant interest-rate environment and no change in the perceived quality of a utility company or its prospects, its stock price should move in parallel with its dividend, as indicated in Table 18.1.

TABLE 18.1 Price Effect of Rising Dividends under Stable Interest Rates

Year	Dividend Rate	Interest Rate	Implied Price
1	$1.00	5%	$20.00
2	$1.06	5%	$21.20
3	$1.12	5%	$22.40
4	$1.18	5%	$23.60
5	$1.24	5%	$24.80

Here, the dividend rate rose by 6% in year 2, driving an equal rate of increase in the stock price. But suppose instead that interest rates rise in year 2, and, worse yet, rise even more in year 3.

Year	Dividend Rate	Interest Rate	Implied Price	One Year Total Return
1	$1.00	5%	$20.00	5.0%
2	$1.06	5.3% (up 6%)	$20.00	5.3%
3	$1.12	5.83% (up 10%)	$19.21	1.65%
4	$1.18	5%	$23.60	28.9%
5	$1.24	5.5%	$22.55	0.8%

TABLE 18.2 Combined Price Effects of Rising Dividend Rates and Fluctuating Interest Rates

As shown in Table 18.2, if interest rates rise by as much as the dividend rate does, the utility stock's price (as in year 2) would remain unchanged. But in a more unfavorable turn of events, as in year 3, suppose interest rates rise faster than the dividend does. In this case rates rose by 10% (from 5.3% to 5.83%). Despite a dividend increase, the stock price declined. This is because rates (the divisor in the fraction) rose more than the dividend (the numerator). The same combination is shown in year 5. In the best of all circumstances, the dividend rate rises *and* the interest rate falls (year 4), combining to propel a sharp stock-price gain.

Since utility stocks generally cannot be expected to increase their dividends by much more than 5% to 6% per year, and since interest rates tend to fluctuate by perhaps 10% to 20% per year, the case for selling in the face of rising interest rates (just before years 3 and 5) is compelling. Simply stated: if interest rates are to rise, they will very likely do so by more than the dividend rate will over the short term, and therefore the stock's price will decline.

Moving out of utility stocks because of changes in interest rates will prove to be more of an art than a science in the real world. First, the investor should understand that selling at the exact price top is a highly unrealistic objective. It should be dismissed and not be allowed to be a source of worry. Second, stock price fluctuations sometimes mask the early stages of a change of expectations about interest rates. Usually the markets can sense changes in business and political conditions and thus anticipate Fed moves to change rates, so utility shares may have already begun to decline before the Fed actually raises the discount rate.

But an inability to pinpoint bottoms in rates (tops in prices) should not become a rationalization for doing nothing. Changes in the discount rate by the Fed's board of governors are powerful signals that should not be ignored—just as changes in dividend policy by the utility's board of directors cannot be. Earlier it was noted that the discount rate is the easiest and most reliable of the signals on interest rates for investors to follow. Monthly data on inflation fluctuate quite a bit and can be distorted by short-term moves in individual components such as food or energy. It can take many months to see that a trend change has occurred, and in the interim there will be both up and down aberrations that lead to confusion.

Likewise, various barometers of business conditions, reported monthly, seldom give smooth readings. Which do you watch: capacity utilization, purchasing managers' intentions, consumer confidence, the unemployment rate, retail sales, consumer credit outstanding, new incorporations, business failures? These indicators often move up one month and down the next; one can contradict the other in any given month. Even the overall Index of Leading Economic Indicators, with its 12 components, often wiggles from month to month. Which signal is the "real" one that must be followed? You cannot tell for a certainty, until after the fact. But you can execute transactions only in real time, not in hindsight.

As a signal for utility stock prices, the discount rate is different from those economic indicators. First, it is a discrete signal, decisively and deliberately given by a policy-making group. Second, and most important in terms of usefulness, the signal rarely wiggles against the prevailing trend. Seldom does the Fed change its collective mind for just a short period. Almost always a change in direction lasts for some time, rather than being reversed in short order. False signals, i.e., single moves in the discount rate not followed by another change in the same direction, are downright rare. How rare? From 1945 through 1992, there were only a handful of changes in discount rate that were not followed by further moves in the same direction: down in 1967; up in 1971; up, then down again, in 1980; up in 1984 (note that the last three occurred in presidential election years).

What this rarity means is that changes in the discount rate are serious business in virtually all cases—signals that cannot be ignored. And, as shown earlier, since changes in the prevailing interest rate usually swamp short-term changes in dividends in terms of relative size, interest-rate changes are the more powerful force driving utility stock prices. And shifts in interest rates tend to be relatively long-lived. In the thirty years from 1962 through 1992, there were just three periods of rising discount rates: 1962-1969; 1972-1975; and 1977-1981. Not only were the moves long, they were major.

TABLE 18.3 Extent of Upward Trends in Discount Rate			
Up-Cycle Dates	Low to High Rate Move	Rate Rose by	Implied Annual Dividend Growth Rate to Offset
1962-1969	3% to 6%	100%	14%
1972-1975	4.5% to 8%	78%	21%
1977-1981	5% to 13%	160%	27%

Note the large percentage figures in the final column of Table 18.3. These are the annual compounded rates by which dividends would have needed to grow during the up-cycles in interest rates for utility stock prices merely to remain unchanged while the Fed was raising the discount rate. Those rates of dividend increase simply do not happen on a sustained basis. Those kinds of increases occur only briefly, during phases when individual companies are restoring dividends after an omission. Those rates will never apply to portfolios of multiple utility stocks at the same time. The implication is clear: good selection — and de-selection—of individual stocks is important but not fully sufficient for truly superior long-term results. Getting out of the way when the Federal Reserve Board says rates will move higher is also highly important. In the nearly fifty years since World War II ended, there have been only three brief false upticks in the discount rate: in 1971, 1980, and 1984. All other first-time upward changes were valid signals that investors lost money by ignoring.

At any time in the market for utility stocks, there will be a list of companies qualifying as buy candidates based on the master signal system provided in Chapter 14. Healthy companies with strong and consistent dividend-growth patterns will be fairly comfortable holdings even while interest rates drift up slightly. But when rates rise significantly, as they have consistently done in recent decades' up-cycle phases, even the best of utility shares will suffer in price. The buying list should be kept ready for the time when the Fed shifts the signal from red to green. In periods of rising rates, ideally only the most dramatic of dividend signals by boards of directors would prompt a current buy action. Ironically, as discussed in earlier chapters, that means that only outright dividend omissions imply that buying is well timed in the face of rising interest rates. Less dramatic positive signals such as accelerated or consistent dividend growth, can be acted upon later, when rates are lowered by the Fed.

Willingness to sell stocks—even those intended as solid long-term investments—at major upturns in interest rates signaled by the Fed is good for another reason: taxes. Too often, a large unrealized capital gain gets in the investor's way psychologically. The larger the gain, the greater the reluctance to sell (both because the investor has grown so fond of the stock and because the tax liability has gotten large). The larger the gain, the deeper must be the drop in price in order to compensate for the reduction in capital that will occur due to payment of the capital gains tax. Therefore, if investors sell utility stocks whenever the Fed raises the discount rate they will be paying small installments of taxes on a pay-as-you-go basis. They will be less likely to resist the Fed's important "sell" signal because of a huge overhanging tax liability.

The best advice is to take your profits when either dividend-policy changes or discount-rate signals dictate, and pay your taxes accordingly along the way. Who knows in advance how deep the drop in stock price will be? Don't let the tax bugaboo become a rationalization for inaction when sales are signaled. Getting accustomed to paying taxes, much as one may dislike the actual paying, is a good investment policy. There will always be another opportunity to buy the stock back lower, or to buy a better stock. Make it a habit to follow important signals. And interest-rate cycle changes defined by Fed discount-rate decisions are definitely among them.

NINETEEN

Earlier we focused on the importance of following rather than ignoring signals provided by the board of directors. Stated simply, dividend policy sends an important message. But this type of change, which analysts would classify as fundamental information, is sometimes foreshadowed by an early message from the market itself—technical information. The particular information of interest is—and this term is not in common usage —relative yield. The relative yield is simply the actual yield of a particular stock compared mathematically with the average yield, or with the band of highest and lowest yields, of a peer group. A given stock's yield should not be judged in isolation over time, since it will be influenced to move up or down by the general level of interest rates. So, a stock should not be considered to have become safer just because its yield has dropped over time from 10% to 8%. The context should be what an average of suitably chosen peers has done. If their average yield has declined from 10% to 6%, the stock now trading to yield 8% is sounding the high-yield alarm bell.

A better way than using any of the popular utility stock averages is to detect early warning signals from the market by keeping score using a carefully chosen set of peers. One must be careful to guard against selecting comparisons that will merely give a comforting vote of confidence. Rather, the universe of comparables should be preselected at time of purchase and then not changed. Telephone stocks should be compared internally, with the Baby Bells in one group and all other local-service providers considered separately. Long-distance carriers (AT&T, GTE,

Sprint) are yet another distinct cluster (MCI Communications pays a nominal dividend, so its yield is meaningless). Natural gas stocks form their own two groups, divided as between distribution companies (local) and transmission pipelines (regional/national). Among electric utilities, there are several key factors:

- nuclear or not
- acid-rain sensitive or not
- multi-state or one-state regulation exposure
- pure electric or electric and gas
- growth vs. mature locations
- history of dividend growth rates

As examples, relative yields should be tracked over time for groups of truly comparable companies. The following are a few possible clusters:

- AlaTenn Resources, Atlanta Gas Light, Berkshire Gas, Brooklyn Union Gas, Connecticut Energy, Peoples Energy, Providence Energy

- Cincinnati Bell, Lincoln Telecommunications, Rochester Telephone, Southern New England Telecom

- Boston Edison, Philadelphia Electric, Detroit Edison, Con Edison of NY, Centerior, Cincinnati Gas & Electric

- Southern Company, Texas Utilities, San Diego G&E, SCEcorp, Nevada Power, SCANA, Florida Progress

- Portland General Electric, TECO, Baltimore G&E, Potomac Electric, Maine Public Service, St. Joseph L&P, IPALCO

Respectively, these groups represent local gas distribution; small-territory telephone companies; mature northern-cities electrics; Sunbelt growth-area electrics; and small-service-area electrics. Other clusters could be created to reflect a truly fair comparison with the particular company of interest. Among electric companies, for example, one should compare nuclear power providers among themselves and multi-state companies among themselves.

Whatever type of utility is being monitored, it is important to *construct a peer group not predominantly from a single state.* Why? Adverse shifts in local regulation would affect all the peer stocks roughly in parallel; by looking at this sample one would miss the market's message that there is trouble brewing in that state, since no one stock's yield would move against the pack (see Table 19.1).

TABLE 19.1 Yield (Percent) on Latest Known Dividend

		Jun88	Sep 88	Dec88	Mar89	Jun89	Sep89	Dec89	Mar 90
Atlanta Gas Lt	ATG	6.64	6.61	6.97	7.60	7.16	6.93	6.45	6.67
Berkshire Gas	BGAS	8.26	8.26	7.11	7.88	7.42	7.64	7.76	8.39
Brooklyn Union	BU	6.95	6.95	7.17	7.49	6.41	6.19	5.63	6.08
Conn. Energy	CNE	5.27	5.61	5.48	8.13	7.95	6.97	6.97	7.39
Peoples Energy	PGL	7.85	8.16	7.75	7.41	6.70	7.40	6.12	7.07
Providence Engy	PVY	5.81	7.27	7.62	8.24	7.78	7.78	7.62	7.94
UGI Corp	UGI	7.29	7.87	7.39	6.78	6.19	5.82	5.92	6.16
Washington Gas	WGL	7.60	7.30	7.60	7.56	7.03	6.97	6.27	6.70
Ave.Yield: Group of 8		6.96	7.25	7.14	7.64	7.08	6.96	6.59	7.05
		Jun90	Sep 90	Dec90	Mar91	Jun91	Sep91	Dec91	Mar92	Jun92
Atlanta Gas Lt	6.56	6.48	6.66	6.53	6.33	6.04	5.75	6.40	5.78
Berkshire Gas	9.14	8.53	8.39	7.76	8.31	7.45	7.45	6.97	7.71
Brooklyn Union	6.51	6.48	6.29	6.76	6.82	6.41	6.15	6.87	6.33
Conn. Energy	8.26	7.50	7.80	7.80	7.23	6.66	6.16	5.91	5.72
Peoples Energy	7.86	7.22	7.03	6.92	6.88	6.81	6.62	6.90	6.70
Providence Engy	8.06	9.03	8.75	8.89	8.75	8.42	8.55	7.14	6.35
UGI Corp	6.12	7.37	6.89	6.74	6.70	6.20	6.09	7.24	7.04
Washington Gas	6.86	6.92	7.00	7.03	7.40	6.46	6.22	6.72	5.90
Ave.Yield: Group of 8	7.42	7.44	7.35	7.30	7.30	6.81	6.62	6.77	6.44

One should track yields on at least an annual basis, and preferably at quarterly intervals or even monthly. Ideally the work should be done in advance of the scheduled dividend meeting so any trouble being flagged by market action can lead to advance rather than reactive measures: selling *before* the possible bad news. Take an average yield of all companies in the chosen group, as was done in Table 19.1, and then compare the yield of the company of interest. The relative yield (to the average, to the high in the group, or to the low) can be computed as follows:

$$\text{Relative yield} = \frac{\text{Dividend yield of stock studied}}{\text{Average, high, or low, for Group}} \times 100$$

The result is expressed as a percentage figure, such as 95% or 120%. Moderate fluctuations of a few points should be considered simply as statistical noise. But jumps of ten points or so, or sustained increases over a few quarters, should act as warnings.

TABLE 19.2 Yields Relative to Average for Group of Eight (Average = 100)

		Jun88	Sep 88	Dec88	Mar89	Jun89	Sep89	Dec89	Mar 90
Atlanta Gas Lt	ATG	95	91	98	99	101	100	98	95
Berkshire Gas	BGAS	119	114	100	103	105	110	118	119
Brooklyn Union	BU	100	96	100	98	91	89	85	86
Conn. Energy	CNE	76	77	77	106	112	100	106	105
Peoples Energy	PGL	113	112	109	97	95	106	93	100
Providence Engy	PVY	84	100	107	108	110	112	116	113
UGI Corp	UGI	105	108	104	89	87	84	90	87
Washington Gas	WGL	109	101	106	99	99	100	95	95
		Jun90	Sep 90	Dec90	Mar91	Jun91	Sep91	Dec91	Mar92	Jun92
Atlanta Gas Lt		88	87	91	89	87	89	87	95	90
Berkshire Gas		123	115	114	106	114	109	112	103	120
Brooklyn Union		88	87	86	93	93	94	93	101	98
Conn. Energy		111	101	106	107	99	98	93	87	89
Peoples Energy		106	97	96	95	94	100	100	102	104
Providence Engy		109	121	119	122	120	124	129	106	99
UGI Corp		82	99	94	92	92	91	92	107	109
Washington Gas		92	93	95	96	101	95	94	99	92

In Table 19.2 several small-area gas distribution utilities are compared. One can detect several noteworthy shifts within the four-plus years of quarterly data shown. For example, Providence Energy (formerly Providence Gas) telegraphed its pending dividend cut, which was finally made early in 1992. Although the directors had failed to declare any further increases after March 1988, it was not until about September 1990 and through 1991 that the relative yield began sending out strong warnings by rising to the 120+ range. Once the dividend was cut, the relative yield moved back into the pack, with readings of 99-106.

Of somewhat more concern to investors as of early 1993 might be Berkshire Gas. Despite having already instituted a modest dividend cut (from $1.28 to $1.08 annually), the stock had begun drifting down enough so its relative yield at mid-1992 seemed to be signaling possible further trouble. But a more positive contrast exists for Connecticut Energy—another company located physically quite near both Berkshire and Providence. After drifting upward into 1990, at the time this study was completed CNE's relative yield had moved lower in its peer-group band for over two years. Further down the Atlantic seaboard, Washington Gas Light remained among the healthier companies in this peer sample throughout the period—and in fact drifted toward the low relative yield for several of the later quarters. That would be a comforting signal to holders.

Figure 19:1 Washington Gas Light, Quarterly Yeild.

An investor following relative-yield signals can plot the data in terms of raw percentage yields on graph paper, as is illustrated in the accompanying plot for Washington Gas Light, whose relative status had been improving from mid-1989 onward (see Figure 19.1). Sometimes relatively sharp changes in all companies' yields during a quarter or two will visually mask the relative movement of one stock. This is why it is usually preferable to perform the relative yield calculation and to plot the results on a scale centered around 100%.

A second possible use of the concept of relative yield is sometimes helpful in considering the merits of different kinds of utility companies. Here, the key to watch for is a change in the historical relationship of electric, gas, telephone, and water stocks' yields. This can be used in either of two ways: individually or as sector averages of many stocks. A highly useful observation was available in late 1989 and early 1990 when telephone stocks dove well below their usual relationships with other groups. The driving force was a near mania to play the cellular business through phone companies. The stocks rallied all out of proportion to the likely effects of the cellular business, cable TV links, and other new applications of communications technology. Yields on telephone stocks dropped to levels well out of line relative to historic norms. The stocks were overpriced,only to come back to earth again. Investors could have used relative yield in a timely manner to avoid new buying or to move funds into other utility sectors.

A third possible use of the relative-yield methodology is in looking at different kinds of companies operating in the same jurisdiction. An example might be to track and then plot the relative yields of NYNEX (telephone), E'town Corp. (water), South Jersey Industries (gas), and either Atlantic Energy or Public Service Enterprises (electric)—all doing business in New Jersey. Any notable drift in relative yield might be a clue to changing relative risk of a specific company.

If the company's stock you hold or are considering buying develops a pattern of meaningfully rising relative yield, a caution flag is being waved at you. Such a warning should never be ignored. It very often predicts trouble ahead for the dividend. And trouble for the dividend also means significant impairment to the investor's capital. Do not tolerate the risk of being cut by this mean two-edged sword! Always keep in mind the time value of money and the cumulative results of lost capital. And remember that your risk tolerance is low and a game of "chicken" is not your style.

The relatively low transaction costs involved in making a switch to a more solidly situated company are very inexpensive insurance against the possibility of a serious financial setback. And the exercise of being decisive and selling a stock without an emergency already having developed will increase your set of investor skills and raise your self-confidence level.

PART FOUR

ISSUES AND TACTICS

Much academic work surrounding the investment markets deals with proving whether and to what extent the markets are "efficient." This concept refers to the degree to which information is known, disseminated, and reflected in prices. Theory holds that an efficient market exists when information is widespread on an equal-access basis and where there are many participants; the combination makes for a liquid market in which prices are set knowledgeably by the continuous action of informed buyers and sellers.

Not all markets are efficient. And some individual markets are more efficient at certain times than at others. Knowing this can help the investor in two ways. First, awareness of the conditions in which markets are less than efficient can help you to avoid problems, much as knowing a street helps in steering around the potholes. Second, being aware of market inefficiencies can contribute to investment results for the investor who, in a disciplined way, actually takes advantage of those inefficiencies. This chapter's purpose is to describe sources of inefficiency and to indicate how they can be used to your advantage.

SIZE: A PRIMARY DETERMINANT OF MARKET EFFICIENCY

The greatest single factor in determining whether a market is efficient is how large that market is. Very simply, as more people and institutions are involved, there is less chance that prices will fail to reflect true value (fundamental inefficiency) or will temporarily swing too widely for lack of opposing bids and offers (technical inefficiency). Market size, or "depth," as some professionals describe it, can provide investors a short-term advantage in the form of good liquidity for market-order executions. Extensive research has documented that over reasonable periods (several years and longer) the returns from investing in small-company stocks regularly exceed those from investing in large-company equities. The main reason for this is that smaller companies are not as well known nor followed as widely by investment analysts (information inefficiency). Therefore, there is a relative lack of demand for their shares, which tend for this reason to sell at discounts to their true value relative to larger companies' stocks.

Probably the key driver of this phenomenon is today's institutional dominance in the market. If a utility (or any other) company has only one million shares outstanding, and if most institutions would prefer not to exceed a 5% position (50,000 shares, in this example) it becomes uneconomic for those institutions to devote salary and travel expense of their analysts to covering the company. Think of Fidelity Management & Research, for example. The Boston-based funds giant had, as of late 1992, some 198 mutual funds with $197 billion under management. So its average fund was $1 billion. Since it is impractical to hold more than perhaps 200 stocks in a portfolio, this implied a minimum $5-million position per stock. So small companies simply cannot be practically considered in such circumstances.

This tendency to concentrate in larger-capitalization issues may well be more pronounced among utility shares, where the popular perception is that the returns available will vary only moderately from one to another. Therefore managers of investment research budgets, believing there is little potential added advantage to having more information, will tend to divert research time and expense away from the industry and especially away from its smaller member companies. According to recent surveys by the Electric Power Research Institute, institutions collectively hold only about 36% of utility common stocks—less than overall market totals. This implies smooth markets in big stocks with tens of thousands of individual owners.

Small-capitalization issues, therefore, may offer the individual investor opportunities for slightly above-average returns. While there will be a relative lack of published research opinion, as discussed earlier in this volume the key information—the dividend growth trend—is easily known; this is the primary driver of the intelligent utility investor's buy/hold/sell/avoid decisions. Where are small-cap stocks most frequently found? Generally not on the New York Stock Exchange, where the minimum standards for initial listing are about $60 million in market value plus some 2,000 holders of at least 100 shares each. Smaller-cap stocks are more frequently found on the American Stock Exchange and on the NASDAQ market. Regional pipelines, small local gas distribution companies, and small-area electric and water companies are commonly listed here rather than on the NYSE.

A good way of checking relative size and overlooked status is to look in the *Monthly Stock Guide* published by Standard & Poor's (many libraries and brokerage firms make these available). Look at the number of shares outstanding and multiply by price. If the result is under $150 million or so, this is probably a neglected stock. Then look for confirmation in the data on institutional holdings and holders. Fewer than about 50 institutions and less than 10% to 15% of the shares in institutional hands will confirm the hypothesis of neglect. This is good news, and for two reasons. First, neglect probably means moderate underpricing (which implies a higher yield than would otherwise be available). And second, low institutional participation means a reduced chance of wide price swings driven by a portfolio managers' stampede if there is ever bad news. Remember the pounding IBM took in December 1992 when it announced 25,000 layoffs and concern about maintaining its dividend? That was caused by institutions all trying to sell at the same time.

Small stocks do not have this hidden risk. Of course, when investing in a small stock, it is important not to own too big a position, or you could find you have trapped yourself when the time to sell comes. Check the average daily volume of trading, available in the *Monthly Stock Guide* and in chart services, or check the Sunday papers for weekly trading totals. You don't want to own as much as a full day's average trading!

An overlooked, smaller utility can provide a modestly higher yield —perhaps a half percent or so—than a company with similar fundamentals that is larger and that trades on the NYSE. After a bear market, when interest rates are high and investors are scared, the advantage can grow even wider for those willing to explore in the shadows. This is not, however, a general endorsement of investing only in AMEX and NASDAQ stocks: they must have the positive dividend-growth attributes described in earlier chapters to qualify as buys. And when they fail to keep increasing dividends at the usual pace, they must be sold, for the slight yield advantage is irrelevant once the board of directors gives a warning signal by changing dividend policy.

TRANSIENT MARKET INEFFICIENCIES: OPPORTUNITIES FOR THE NIMBLE

Relative size is a somewhat enduring characteristic contributing to market inefficiency and thus potential investor advantage. But there are also several temporary circumstances that can offer a chance to profit for those on the lookout. These all have in common the temporary imbalance of buying demand and selling supply. The sophisticated investor wants to be on the smaller side of the market—buying into a temporary oversupply or selling into a burst of buying. Some of the most common opportunities arise in connection with the following:

* dividend timing
* tax-loss selling
* year-end partnership avoidance
* dividend-reinvestment plan effects
* big moves on slow-trading days
* unimportant news
* stock distributions creating excess supply

These will each be described briefly. In each case, the simplest formula to remember is to take action on the opposite side from the one temporarily dominating the market.

As described in Chapter 23, there is a tendency among investors to hold a stock until after the ex-dividend date and sell it thereafter. The illogic of that practice earned it an entire chapter.

Here, suffice to say the smart investor would prefer to be a seller into the run-up just before the ex-dividend date and would be a buyer several days after that time when the stock has been driven lower by others' selling. These, of course, are merely short-term *tactics,* since the major buy/sell decision is based on the six conditions outlined in Chapter 14.

Tax-loss selling effects provide some very interesting opportunities for utilities investors following the buy/sell system presented in this book. Why? Buying on the ultimate bad news (an omitted dividend) is a contrarian strategy. Stocks whose dividends have been omitted will be sold down heavily and typically will again come under year-end tax-selling pressure. Such selling depresses the price temporarily and provides a good tactical entry point. The period of tax selling may start as early as mid-November, although in earlier times it reputedly was concentrated in late December only. The tax-selling season represents a temporary market inefficiency in that for a brief time there are abnormal numbers of sellers whose motive for selling will end at a known time. Tax-loss selling is most acute among losing stocks in years when the market has risen, since investors try to balance losses against earlier gains to reduce taxes. The tendency is less pronounced, although never absent, in down-market years. Possible or planned changes in the tax laws can also create temporary tax-driven market trends.

For example, as was anticipated in early 1993, when there is a chance that the new year will bring higher marginal tax brackets, gains will be taken late in the old year and losses early in the new one. The opposite, of course, is true whenever a tax cut occurs. Whatever the immediate circumstances, the tactically alert investor will attempt to be on the opposite side of the temporary effect, late into the affected period. Again, this is tactical advice which assumes the presence of appropriate buy/sell fundamentals as defined earlier.

Because of certain provisions in the IRS code providing favorable tax status to energy-related enterprises, some energy pipelines are structured as limited partnerships (LPs). Being a partner by buying shares means the investor has a more complex task at income tax time than does a corporate dividend recipient who merely copies the amounts shown on his or her 1099-DIV forms.

Therefore, many investors hesitate to own partnerships. This bias in itself contributes to systematic underpricing and therefore the opportunity for a yield advantage. But a second aspect of partnership avoidance also occurs annually and to a lesser extent at the end of quarters and months.

Suppose you are attracted to a certain LP in the gas transmission business. It is December, and you realize that holding off until January will save you a more complex tax return filing in April. You may postpone buying until the new year. Similarly, some holders inclined to sell out may want to end their partnership status before the new year starts to avoid another complex filing a year from April. They will tend to be sellers in December. The result is a temporary time imbalance of buyers and sellers; this inefficiency in the market can offer opportunities for savvy buyers and pitfalls for unsophisticated sellers. Similar but smaller effects occur at the ends of months and quarters. These relate to how often the partnership reviews its holder list to assign proportional income for tax purposes. Sellers and buyers may time their actions with this in mind, causing temporary price fluctuations.

Some dividend-reinvestment plans (DRPs)—which are discussed in some detail in Chapter 24—have quarterly effects on a stock's price action. This occurs when the plan agent goes into the market to buy shares, thus creating temporarily increased demand. If you own and are planning to sell shares of a utility soon after it has given a negative-momentum dividend signal, this bulge of buying may provide an excellent exit point. It is important to have on file a copy of the DRP prospectus, which will describe in detail when the quarterly reinvestments actually will occur.

You should also look in the annual report to check how big the effect may be. This can be done by examining the cash-flow statement, which will show how much money was captured in the form of reinvested dividends in the prior year. If it is a small percentage of total dividends paid, and if the stock is highly active anyway, the price effect may be invisible. A strong clue will come from the terms of the plan: the more attractive the terms (discounted price, no fees or commissions), the more likely it is that the participation will be widespread among holders.

Slow-trading days can provide welcome opportunities if you are planning to be a seller or buyer anyway. Examples of slow days include Columbus Day, Veterans' Day, Yom Kippur, and the Monday after Easter (a holiday in Europe), the two days surrounding Thanksgiving, the day before or after Christmas, the Friday before Labor Day, and any other days that could be part of unofficial extended weekends when a holiday falls on a Tuesday or Thursday.

If because of the news background there happens to be a strong move in the market, either up or down, two effects are likely. First, on the slow day itself there is a better chance than normal that a limit order a little away from the prior close might get filled. For example, you might more easily buy down 1/2 or 3/4 of a point than on most other days. Second, there is a strong likelihood that the market day following a sharp move on light trading will bring a reversal of direction. If you are planning to be a seller, you might do best in the early morning after a big up-move on light volume, for example.

Unimportant news usually offers the disciplined contrarian investor a short-term tactical opportunity. Typical types of passing news providing nimble utility investors extra returns are usually adverse events. A telephone system failure, a gas explosion, an earthquake in the service territory, or a hurricane shutting down electric service are classic examples. Bear in mind that these are all a part of doing business. Sure, earnings in the quarter will be hurt a few cents per share due to repair costs. But a warm winter or cool summer would have a similar effect, except that it would be less dramatic or sudden in investors' consciousness. The devastation of Hurricane Andrew in Florida during the fall of 1992 provided a temporary decline in shares of FPL, TECO, and Florida Progress; investors wanting to buy anyway would have gained a point or more by bravely buying in the full knowledge that life would go on as before. SCEcorp and Pacific Gas & Electric provide periodic examples of temporary market inefficiencies whenever there is a medium-sized earthquake in California.

Similarly, watch NYNEX and AT&T for opportunity when there is a phone failure in New York City. Shortly before publication time, Hawaiian Electric announced it was exiting the insurance business in the wake of losses in the islands caused by Hurricane Iniki in late 1992. The market sold HE down several points despite the objective conclusion that the company would be at lower risk in the future. This was an excellent example of a temporary market inefficiency providing opportunity.

Major stock distributions and spin-offs, although relatively rare, provide classic examples of temporarily inefficient markets. Therefore, they can provide significant opportunities. When a company spins off one or more of its businesses to shareholders by giving them stock in two companies instead of one, often one of the resulting entities becomes a temporary "orphan" in the market. Many shareholders view the distribution as an unexpected "extra dividend" and sell it when received since they have no real interest in being a long-term holder. The obvious implication: this is an opportunity for the nimble. It is important to watch trading volume until it quiets down significantly, indicating that the period of selling pressure is finished; impatient buying earlier in the process would be foolish.

A rather unusual example of another kind of distribution occurred in Tucson Electric Power in December 1992. TEP had gone through a near-bankruptcy process in which it liquidated much of its debt and all of its preferred stock by issuing 135 million new shares of common stock to their holders. Bankers and preferred holders had no interest in becoming owners of a low-priced common stock that had paid no dividends since 1989 and showed little prospect of an early resumption of payments. So they unloaded their new common shares as soon as they received them.

The stock had traded in the $3.50-$4 range shortly before the distribution and dove to $1 at the height of the selling wave. Coming in December, which would be tax-selling season anyway for a depressed stock (its old high before dividend growth stopped was $65!), this new supply of stock provided a short-term opportunity to buy for at least a trade. The stock bounced to $2.50 in two weeks. (The stock was "cleaned out" technically but, with annual revenues in the range of $3 per share, arguably it had quickly become fundamentally fully priced at $3 unless one wants to count on the long-term takeover value of its excess nuclear plant capacity in the hands of another holder with greater generation-capacity needs.)

SUMMARY AND CONCLUSION

This chapter has described both long-term and temporary types of market inefficiency that can be used by the investor to tactical advantage. However, it is important to focus on the basic signals for buying and selling as the primary reasons for taking action; these inefficient-market opportunities should be viewed only as tactical tools for short-term advantage. They should not lure the informed utilities investor into undesirable situations just because an apparent short-term "bargain" may be perceived. While investors should resist becoming traders, they can and should still use wise traders' tactics for good timing and execution of their long-term strategic moves.

TWENTY-ONE

Potential investors in electric power companies face a question unique to this part of the utilities landscape, for only here are there choices of fuel source. The issue is whether to invest in nuclear power or not. For the many people who have established their attitudes toward nuclear power (whether on a rational basis or otherwise), there really is no question. To oppose the use of nuclear power clearly implies boycotting an investment in companies that produce it. For those who either favor nuclear power generation or remain ambivalent, the issue is more nearly a simple investment question involving relative risks and rewards. This chapter outlines those investment considerations and provides a listing of electric power companies which have no present nuclear capacity and none under construction.

THE REWARDS

Since the near-catastrophic nuclear plant accident at Three Mile Island (TMI) in March 1979, electric utilities with nuclear power participation have traded at yields exceeding those for non-nuclear companies. Cognizant of the high level of public and investor concern over the issue, analysts and investment reference and advisory services include mentions of nuclear status in virtually all discussions of individual electric utility stocks. This keeps the issue alive and helps to perpetuate the yield differential.

The principal reward from investing in a utility company utilizing nuclear power is that its yield is likely to be higher than that of a comparably situated company with no nuclear participation. It is difficult to state exactly what yield difference is caused strictly by the nuclear factor since others (size, capitalization structure, quality of management, and so on) make any comparison of companies less a science than an art. However, as of late 1992 the current-yield advantage was about 0.6%. This figure was derived by averaging all the yields of nonnuclear electric utilities and comparing the result with that for all nuclear electric utilities. (In each case, utilities paying no dividends and those selling at very low yields after having recently resumed dividends were excluded.)

A potential second reward for investing in nuclear electric utility companies might be a continued closing of the relative yield gap over time. For example, as of late 1988 the average yield differential was a full 1%. A decade ago, when the specter of TMI was fresh in the media and in the minds of investors, the yield differential was much wider, averaging over 2.0%. Thus it appears that this possible reward has already largely been enjoyed in the past, since it seems unlikely that the gap will close entirely.

A third potential advantage of investing in nuclear operators is that at some time in the future the economic/political/regulatory/psychological climate might turn more in favor of the group. A new oil embargo, negative environmental shifts regarding coal, or a major and sustained rise in the price of natural gas might tilt the balance more favorably toward nuclear. But it appears that the fear of a nuclear accident—one that was made very real even with what little the American public knows about Chernobyl—is unlikely ever to allow our society to develop a warm and cozy feeling about nuclear energy.

THE RISKS

The greatest risk from investing in nuclear energy generating utilities is, of course, that of a nuclear accident. The stock of General Public Utilities, parent of the operator of TMI, dropped 50% in two months from the date of the accident and eventually—in 15 months—dropped 80% before hitting bottom. And that nuclear event was "only" a *near*-catastrophe.

The financial risk of owning a nuclear electric utility extends beyond the direct effects of a possible event at its facilities, however. The Price-Anderson Act imposes a mutual-insurance scheme on the industry, exposing every nuclear operator to potential liability of $560 million in the case of a nuclear accident for any one. Even if financial damage were much more limited in an accident, however, the prices of all nuclear electrics' shares would suffer a sinking spell in sympathy and in anticipation of possible added regulatory burdens.

Any time there is a well-publicized "event" at a nuclear power plant, investors in all nuclear electric generators' shares can expect at least a small ripple of price weakness. Memories of TMI are long, and the degree of horror associated with a nuclear accident is high. Such factors drive investment decisions, at least in the short term. Events, as defined by the Nuclear Regulatory Commission (NRC), range from seemingly minor rule infractions, such as improper tool storage, to the ultimate—a meltdown. According to NRC records, despite the increased attention paid to compliance following the TMI accident and despite the presence of at least one full-time NRC inspector at every plant, about a decade later there were still approximately 2,900 incidents nationwide per year, which averages about two per plant per month. Most are minor, but many receive publicity and can affect the stocks' prices. And, even if there is never another accident as bad as that in 1979, the investor is exposed to psychological risk.

For any utilities that have plants still in construction, or still waiting for final approval for operation and inclusion in the rate base, there exists considerable political risk and resulting investor uncertainty as the slow process evolves. Public authorities are not ruled by the logic of the marketplace, and sometimes the sway of public opinion can cause unfair decisions in the light of 20/20 hindsight. Plants have been approved for construction only to be later declared partly or entirely "excess capacity" by the same commissions when later power demand fell short of forecasts approved by those commissions. As a result, billions of dollars have been excluded from the rate base.

Commonwealth Edison and Public Service of New Mexico are examples. Companies which have, either by the decisions of their directors or under orders or pressure from regulatory commissions, abandoned nuclear investments continue to face uncertainty over the degree to which recovery through rates will be allowed. Until the amounts of such recoveries are finally established, even some "nonnuclear" companies face a residue of uncertainty from their nuclear pasts.

The seriousness of the regulatory risk is illustrated by the fate of dividends among nuclear electric utilities: no less than 11 of the 14 highest-yielding nuclear companies—as of the end of 1988— had cut or eliminated their dividends within the ensuing four years! While it may be argued that this was a period of maximum regulatory overhang, that observation is of little consolation to holders whose incomes and portfolios were melted as a result of owning high-yield nuclear utilities. Because the economic scale of a minimum nuclear plant investment is so huge, the financial impact of an adverse regulatory result is usually quite severe for these companies.

A real but unquantifiable political risk exists: a future generation of national leadership could adopt a militantly anti-nuclear position and exert pressure on the industry, which would cause losses for investors. The possible types of pressure range from more onerous and costly compliance requirements all the way, theoretically, to an order to close plants by a certain date.

A more distant risk exists in the form of unknown future costs of waste transport and disposal, and site decontamination. Public Service Company of Colorado, which owns at Fort St. Vrain a nuclear station of the Chernobyl design, has shut down the facility but faces such unquantifiable costs. Further down the road, when existing plants are determined to be obsolete and must be retired, their operators will face similar questions. The first U.S. nuclear plant was contracted for in 1953, and the last in 1979. The population of 120 plants is aging. The costs of safely deactivating and mothballing old facilities can be expected to be borne more by the stockholders than by the public (rate payers) since the organized populist antinuclear activist lobby is strong and vocal.

SUMMARY: A BALANCED ASSESSMENT OF THE INVESTOR'S RISKS AND REWARDS

This chapter has attempted to steer a middle course by neither condemning nor embracing nuclear power. The purpose has been to assist the reader in identifying the sources of risk and reward, rather than to make judgments about nuclear power.

A dispassionate analysis could lead to a result that one could interpret in either way: the extra yield is, or is not, worth the risk. Given all the risks noted, many of which are unable to be mathematically measured, how can one justify accepting a current yield of only 0.6% more for taking the risk? Or, stated with the opposite bias, given that the yield advantage is about 10% (that is, perhaps 6.6% vs. 6.0%), how can one resist the extra current return, since the chance for a serious accident has so far proven much less than 10% per year?

For what it may be worth, it appears that professional investors have come down on the side of assuming the risk in pursuit of the added return. As of late 1992, according to figures compiled by The Value Line Investment Survey, institutional holdings (as defined by Value Line) were 30% in nuclear-power electric companies on average, against 25.5% in non-nuclear companies. (Holdings in telephone, gas, and water utilities were even higher, and yields for each of those groups were lower, than for electric utilities.)

The choice belongs to each reader. Your author has owned, and will in the future very likely again own, nuclear electric companies' shares. And yet, intuitively, there remains the haunting knowledge that the risk, while remote, is potentially huge—while the relative yield advantage is barely more than half a percent on average. For those who are pathologically averse to risk, such a calculus would be unacceptable. Each of us must, as I quoted Bernard Baruch previously, "invest only up to the sleeping point."

As a convenience to readers, Table 21.1 lists U.S. electric utility companies that had, as of early 1993, no nuclear facilities in use or under construction. For those concerned with geographic diversification, the names are grouped into regions.

TABLE 21.1 List of Non-Nuclear Electric Utilities	
Company Name	Location(s)
CITIZENS UTIL	Diversified
INTERSTATE POWER	Diversified
UTILICORP UNITED	Diversified
ALLEGHENY POWER	Northeast
ORANGE & ROCKLAND	Northeast
DPL INC.	Mid-Atlantic
POTOMAC ELECTRIC	Mid-Atlantic
KU ENERGY	Southeast
LG&E ENERGY	Southeast
TECO ENERGY	Southeast
CENT. LA. ELECT.	South
OKLAHOMA GS & EL	Southwest
SOUTHW'N PUB SVC	Southwest
TNP ENTERPRISES	Southwest
TUCSON ELEC PWR	Southwest
NEVADA POWER	Far West
PACIFICORP	Far West
SIERRA PACIFIC	Far West
IDAHO POWER	Far West
HAWAIIAN ELECTRIC	Pacific
MDU RESOURCES	North Central
MONTANA POWER	North Central
NORTHW'N PUB SVC	North Central
CILCORP INC.	Upper Midwest
CINCINNATI G & E	Upper Midwest
CIPSCO INC.	Upper Midwest
MINNESOTA P & L	Upper Midwest
OTTER TAIL POWER	Upper Midwest
EMPIRE DISTRICT EL	Midwest
IPALCO ENTERPRISES	Midwest
NIPSCO INDUSTRIES	Midwest
PSI RESOURCES	Midwest
SOUTHERN IND. G & E	Midwest
ST. JOE LT & PWR	Midwest

TWENTY-TWO

Avoiding the Trap of Local Investing

Being unable to see the proverbial forest for the trees is a subtle but common investment problem. It applies when the investor is "too close" to the companies he or she has invested in. Such myopia can be generated by a community tie to a major local employer, by a personal or neighbor's employment situation (present or past), by the opinions of respected others who have connections to the company, and by the not-inconsiderable influence of the media and of community groups. These factors can exert either positive or negative biases, sometimes quite powerful ones, on the investor's thinking. And, to compound matters, you can receive intense but conflicting messages at the same time, with the effect of raising the level of confusion. As an example of the latter, the city gas company might be seen in a good light for sponsoring a charitable event at exactly the same time it is being castigated in the local press for charging "unfair" rates to retired citizens.

It would be difficult—and probably seem downright irresponsible —for a writer to suggest that an investor should try to be distant and ignorant concerning the facts about his or her investments. We all have a tendency to play armchair detective and to want to comb over any available information about the industries and companies in which our money is invested. This becomes an even greater tendency when the investor is retired and has additional time to spend reading, attending public meetings, and so on. However, this author's bias is in favor of maintaining some objectivity-building distance when investing in utility companies' securities. The risk of doing otherwise is the likelihood of reacting to well-publicized or dramatic news that will be of little lasting import: one may be so moved by locally reported events as to buy high (on good news) or sell low (on temporary bad news). In psychological terms, the closer one is to the source of the news, the more believable and important it seems — and the more likely one is to lose perspective.

If you own stock in a nearby utility company, you are likely to discover many local fans of that utility who also own its stock or bonds. They will remain loyal beyond when they should, so they will provide you with bad advice when the dividend signal turns negative. They will be looking into their personal rear-view mirrors. Spare yourself this bad counsel. Two ways to do this are to keep your investment business to yourself and to invest *non*-locally.

LOCAL NEWS THAT DOESN'T MATTER

Following are some kinds of news events that not uncommonly surround utility companies, with comments indicating why a fixation on the local news will mar one's investment judgment:

EVENT/OBSERVATION

Major storm disrupts phone/electric service

> Storms should be expected; there is usually some insurance recovery; earnings hit is only temporary.

Gas explosion and fire

> Not rare in earthquake prone areas such as California; if there is no allegation of a pattern of negligence, there is no lasting risk to the investor.

Water/electric company files for rate increase

> Happens frequently; part of the business; neither good nor bad news: they will not get all they ask for.

Citizen/politician outrage over rate request

> Predictable. No one likes to pay higher rates; politicians and antibusiness activists traffic in such protests regularly; the press usually supports the "unfortunate ratepayer." Ignore these circus acts.

Company gets only part of requested rate hike

> Absolutely predictable. So is their official "disappoint-
> ment." Part of the recurring dance.

"Innovative" new business practices used locally

> A better water meter or a new weekend calling discount
> are not likely to be unique to the local company despite
> getting much play in the local press and/or in monthly
> bill stuffers.

Regulatory criticism

> Regulators are paid to regulate and taxpayers feel well
> served when the commission criticizes the usually
> unpopular utility monopoly company for excess
> advertising, executive perks/salaries, or other misdeeds.
> "Monopoly" is a hot word in press coverage. Expect this
> part of the game.

Company self-congratulation for good deeds

> They conserve, sponsor the run for the handicapped,
> teach school kids about safety. This is not new or
> unique. Public relations jobs depend on your knowing
> about it. Does it affect your dividend rate much?

The list could go on and on. The key point for you as an investor
is to maintain a sense of detachment and perspective. Ask yourself whether you'd be surprised if, after moving to another state,
you found that the local gas or phone company there gets into the
local news there for most of the same things. The operative issue
very probably is whether the news is indeed local or actually gets
national play. A reasonably good test for whether news about
your local utility is important is whether it is reported in *The
Wall Street Journal* or any of the national business news maga-
zines. Remember, anything scandalous, such as a cover-up of
safety violations or knowingly pumping tainted water, will
receive such coverage. That tells you management is in trouble,
or will be, with the regulators. Minor, routine developments of
local interest fail to make the national news *because* they are of
no real economic importance. Short of truly significant problems,
the local news will contain little of lasting importance to
investors. Remember, the vast majority of investors never will
even hear, let alone act on, the news you see locally.

KEEPING AN EYE ON WHAT IS IMPORTANT

As was discussed in previous chapters of this book, the most critical investment element surrounding any utility's stock is the growth rate of the dividend, and any change in that growth rate. The board of directors will give you all the important news neatly wrapped up in that little quarterly message. Their dividend decisions reflect an informed overall perspective on company fortunes and prospects. Everything else that occurs between board meetings can be considered relatively minor unless it is covered in the national media. You will be tempted to invest in a local utility company if you see and hear and read good things about it. Those things that are so well-known locally are usually trivial compared with the dividend trend. Then, if you do own a local utility company's shares, you may be scared unnecessarily into selling out on the basis of local publicity over some passing event or controversy.

The best way to avoid being tossed about by the news is to keep a safe distance. The way to do that is to invest *non*-locally. There are over a hundred electric or electric-and-gas companies; about fifty gas transmission and distribution companies, two dozen phone companies, and perhaps a dozen water companies in which you can find attractive investment potentials. You will gain little if anything essential to your investment decisions by focusing on a local company—and you may well be overpowered by an excess of information which has little long-term or big-picture importance.

One good perspective always to use when thinking of buying on good news or selling on bad news (in utility stocks or any others, for that matter) is this: pretend you can travel 10 years into the future. Look back at the current event, and see if it is one of the two or three most strategically or fundamentally critical events of that decade over which you are now looking back. If the answer is anything less than a firm yes, then you should take no investment action in the same direction (positive/negative) as today's news. When you avoid local companies, you will need to spend much less time in these time-travel adventures. You can better spend your time watching the dividends on a nationwide basis, and taking actions accordingly.

Your local utility companies may be gems. But you can find similar ones elsewhere and not risk the loss of clear vision that often accompanies investing in the local ones.

TWENTY-THREE

The Tax Trap: Buying a Dividend

Dividends are built into the prices of stocks. One does not receive a dividend "free" since the market is efficient in marking down prices once a stock has begun trading ex-dividend. So it is surprising how many investors make a tactical error by following a practice called "buying a dividend." It causes cash-balance depletion, accelerates tax liabilities, and often causes real but unnoticed capital losses.

While bonds trade at a quoted price *plus accrued interest to date*, stocks trade with expected dividend payments *included in the price*. If stocks were traded in penny multiples (as mutual funds are) rather than in eighths, there would be a much more nearly perfectly efficient mechanism for reflecting accrued dividend expectations in the stocks' daily prices. For example, imagine a preferred stock or perhaps a highly stable blue-chip common with an annual dividend rate of $3.65 per share. Since dividends are payable quarterly, the stock's price would gradually build in a penny a day, seven cents a week ($0.9125 per calendar quarter) of expected dividends, until the quarterly ex-dividend date. On that day, the new buyer does not get the immediately pending dividend and so would not pay the accumulated 91-cent premium. In a perfectly static market with unchanged interest rates and no shift in perceptions of risk, the stock's price chart would look like a serrated knife blade with a horizontal slope. In such a market, the buyer and seller would be accurately and fairly splitting the per diem accrual of expected dividends: a buyer late in the quarter would pay the seller for nearly a full quarter's dividend and would then receive the whole payment from the company a short time later.

The buyer and seller, however, also are each making choices as to the tax status of the quarter's dividend payment. Suppose the $3.65 preferred described above sells at $40 on its ex-dividend date and gradually creeps up to $40.875 just before the next "ex" date. Ignoring commissions for simplicity, an owner with a cost of perhaps $40 per share can sell for $40.875 just prior to the ex date and record a capital gain of $0.875 per share but will forego the pending dividend income. At various times capital gains have been treated more favorably than dividend income, so in such periods this strategy would be logical to pursue. At *any* time when the holder has an offsetting capital loss and/or a capital-loss carryforward, taking the current quarter's income in the form of a greater capital gain rather than as a dividend has clear positive tax consequences. If the holder literally needs the current income, he or she should withdraw the quarterly amount from the brokerage account. In effect this is "paying" oneself a tax-free amount, rather than accepting the dividend and its 1099-DIV consequences. The holder truly has an option of transforming the latest quarter's nearly fully accrued dividend income into a capital gain (or the reduction of a capital loss).

From the rational buyer's viewpoint, there is clear and even more compelling incentive to postpone purchase until after the ex-dividend date. Why? A pre-ex-date purchase creates a near-term dividend received which unavoidably becomes a part of the current year's tax liability. At the extreme, by buying a day before the stock trades ex, one can receive five dividends while owning the stock for a year and a day, or two for owning for 92 days. But the price of the stock goes down immediately after the purchase, by an amount usually equal to the imminent quarterly payment. That loss in capital has no tax benefit until the transaction is closed out (perhaps *years* later), at which time a higher cost basis exists than if the stock had been bought ex the first dividend. In effect, one has bought the first dividend and paid taxes on it but suffered a paper loss with no tax benefit (yet). The buyer of the quick dividend has accelerated his or her tax liabilities and perhaps turned a capital gain (taxed lower sometimes) into fully taxable dividend income. A further (albeit small) penalty of buying the dividend by paying the higher stock price is that some brokerage commissions are figured on the value of the trade, so one bears a slightly higher cost in this form.

Surprisingly, many investors—in some cases encouraged by their brokers—routinely and out of habit buy dividends, and/or hold past the ex date to get the dividend before selling. This is illogical and in fact tends to create a small opportunity for savvy investors willing to be disciplined and play the game the opposite way. Investors who buy or hold for the "extra income" of a pending dividend tend to push the stock price above its legitimate level just before the ex date (via added buying pressure and withheld supply of selling). And then collectively such investors artificially depress the price (by selling) just afterward. The tactically savvy investor should instead wait (all other price-driving factors held constant) until shortly *after* the ex date to buy into the price weakness thus created.

Some evidence exists that there are opportunities created from this minor market inefficiency, and that these opportunities are self-correcting. When the stock sells ex its latest dividend, its price is lower, and therefore its apparent yield (such as is printed in many newspapers, is carried in screenable databases, or can be readily calculated by armchair investors) is higher at this time of the quarter. This tends to attract "yield-hound" buyers who push the price upward. The effect is to create a quarterly cycle of price fluctuation. It is a pattern in most cases too small to be useful for short-term trading (due to commission costs), but it does offer the savvy utility-stock investor chances for opportune timing of purchases and sales otherwise planned.

The tax-logical tactical approach to buying, or *not buying* a dividend is even more important in the case of mutual funds. Most growth-oriented common-stock mutual funds pay their dividends just once a year, so the amount of the "ex" and the related income payment (which *do* accrue on a daily basis and which *are* exactly equal in the case of an open-ended fund) become large—four times as large as the quarterly event for a utility common stock with the same yield. This facet of mutual funds offers some potentially useful tax-timing opportunities as described above, but on a larger scale, for investors using the funds in taxable accounts. For the many investors who use funds inside their IRA, 401(k), and Keogh plans, of course, the distinction is moot.

Since utilities fund buyers are predominantly income oriented, just about all utility mutual funds (as well as closed-end utilities funds) pay their dividends not annually but rather quarterly or monthly. In this case, the amount of dividend one is buying by acquiring shares in the fund just before an ex date is rather small. But in a taxable portfolio, literally every little bit counts, as becomes evident on April 15.

Another way of looking at the issue of the logical decision on buying a dividend or not is this: think in after-tax terms. Suppose a stock pays $4.00 per year in four quarterly dividends. Suppose you are one day short of the ex-dividend date and are considering purchase of the stock on its merits for the long term. The day before the ex occurs, the potential buyer is faced with perhaps a $50 stock price, but inside that price is embedded a $1.00 (pretax) dividend payable in three or four weeks. Is that $1.00 dividend worth a full dollar? Not to a taxable investor! It is worth, arguably, no more than $0.72 due to just the federal tax liability that the upcoming payment carries with it. But the stock is very likely to open a full dollar lower on the ex-dividend date. So the day-early (that is, the pre-ex-date) buyer is paying $50.00 for a package that will be worth $49.72 a day later. Not a great bargain. Why does the stock tend to trade down a whole dollar?

There are probably three reasons: first, the lore of Wall Street is that dividends imply the full stated amount in price markdown on the ex day; second, the sophisticated taxable buyer is not willing to absorb the seller's tax problem by paying up; third, such a large amount of daily trading of utility shares is in the hands of institutions whose trades are nontaxable events, that those dominant players conduct their actions and make decisions that "set" prices (via supply and demand) on a basis that ignores taxes.

The advice for a savvy individual investor: don't buy a dividend unless there is a compelling reason to expect the stock immediately to rise more than enough to compensate for your tax liability. Such reasons might include a dividend increase not fully expected by the Street, a strong downtrend in interest rates, or soft economic news that will cause a short-term spurt in demand for "safe" stocks and income-oriented issues in general.

TWENTY-FOUR

Using Dividend Reinvestment Plans

This chapter describes dividend reinvestment plans (DRPs) and discusses the many advantages (as well as the few disadvantages) they present to the utility investor. For those readers who have used these plans the chapter is not essential reading, although some review of the positives and negatives may be worth a few minutes' time. While the presence of a DRP is attractive, it should not be a criterion for investment selection. (However, as discussed below, termination of a plan is indeed a valid reason for negative selection—selling or avoiding the stock.)

DESCRIPTION OF THE PLANS

A dividend reinvestment plan (DRP) allows shareholders, on a strictly voluntary basis, to have their dividends automatically invested in additional full and fractional shares of the company. Each plan has its own rules, which are completely and clearly set out in a DRP prospectus; there is often a small brochure that simplifies the language and acts as a handy quick reference. For investors who plan a long-term position in a company, and who do not need current dividend income for living expenses, the DRP is a very attractive means of automatically reinvesting and compounding one's income stream. From the company's viewpoint, the DRP has three virtues:

- It lessens the cash outflow associated with paying dividends (if new shares are issued).

- It tends to support the stock price (if dividends are used to make market purchases of existing shares).

- It tends to create shareholder loyalty through the reinforcing behavior of periodic additional investing.

199

A DRP in a utility (or industrial) company's stock is conceptually identical to that in a mutual fund; readers who own funds and have elected to reinvest their distributions are familiar with the nature of such a plan. For others, a DRP plan may be thought of somewhat (although not identically) as a passbook savings account. The company records on paper, at first, the amount of shares owned by the holder. Each time there is a dividend paid, the dollar value of that dividend, rather than being paid out by check, is credited toward the holder's account in the form of added shares and fractions of shares. The next time a dividend is paid, it is paid on the increased number of shares (including fractions) then held, rather than on only the original shares. The effect is automatic compounding. As with a bank account, there is in almost every DRP a cash-purchase option under which the holder may make voluntary cash contributions to be invested in additional shares. And, in virtually all DRPs, there is also a partial-liquidation option, under which the owner may order any part, but not necessarily all, of his or her shares to be sold and a check for the proceeds mailed out. The major differences between a DRP and a bank account are that the DRP is not insured, and that the bank account is denominated in dollars (each of which will be worth a dollar at all times) while the DRP is denominated in shares (which by definition will fluctuate in dollar value with the market for the stock).

DRPs have various names such as, "Shareholders' Reinvestment and Common Share Purchase Plan," but the format is usually the same. Most have voluntary cash-purchase options (often with frequency or dollar limits). Some charge nominal transaction fees and/or brokerage commissions (typically $0.03 to $0.05 per share); some plans absorb such costs but in that case are required by IRS regulations to report such amounts as added dividend income on the holder's annual 1099. In most plans, sales are made on request as soon as written notice is received.

However, in the large majority of plans voluntary cash purchases are made only once per quarter (coincident with the dividend) or at most once per month. This feature severely limits the investor's ability to time purchases to attractive short-term market opportunities. Some plans issue new shares at small discounts (typically 2% to 5%) against market value (again, the difference must be reported to the IRS as extra dividend income). Discounts are common when the stock sells above its book value. Many plans issue new shares only at such times. When the stock sells below book value, most plans switch from new-share issuance to open-market repurchases. This keeps the company from selling new stock at dilutive below-book values and the buying demand slightly supports the stock price while it is depressed. Virtually all DRPs require that the holder initially own some shares held in physical certificate form (rather than held in street name by the broker); only a few major brokerage firms have set up the computer facilities to allow street-name holders to participate in companies' DRP plans. A small number of plans allow investors to make their initial purchase of shares directly from the company (thus bypassing minimum brokerage commissions); in the case of utility companies this feature is usually limited to residents of the company's home state, or to actual customers.

ADVANTAGES OF DRPs FOR THE INVESTOR

DRPs provide a number of attractive benefits to participants:

- Automatic compounding, which provides discipline and in effect creates dollar cost averaging.
- Low or zero commissions on reinvestment and voluntary transactions.
- In some cases, ability to reinvest dividends at a discount (in effect increasing the value of dividends actually declared).
- Free safekeeping of certificates.
- Low commission costs at time of sale.
- Automatic, concise, computer-accurate record keeping (handy at tax time).
- The required provision of a prospectus to the participant.
- A highly significant signal in case of termination or suspension of the plan. Nonparticipants would usually not learn of this event on a timely basis, if at all.

The last two points are perhaps the most significant in terms of investment decisions. The DRP prospectus must be revised whenever a change is made to the plan itself. But, more important, it must be kept current in terms of significant corporate events and information. This means that if some materially adverse developments are affecting the company, they must be disclosed. Often there will be language that hints at the possibility of future distress to earnings and the ability to continue or increase the dividend. This is a signal the investor should not ignore. It is very strongly recommended that the investor retain past prospectus copies and compare the language with that in new versions to note any changes.

Termination or suspension of a DRP plan should be viewed as a highly alarming event. This occurs when a board of directors will have been advised by its lawyers that offering new shares under distressed circumstances could lead to shareholder lawsuits. If the company is afraid to sell you new shares, it means they think there is news coming that may cause a sharp drop in share price. You may prudently assume that such news means a dividend cut or omission. Therefore, suspension or termination of the DRP plan is a signal to sell your stock promptly.

Even if they do not intend to participate in the DRP, investors considering the purchase of a utility's shares would be well advised to contact the company first and ask for a copy of the DRP prospectus; information in this legally required and S.E.C.-filed offering document is prepared by the attorneys and presented in cautionary tones while the annual report with its glossy photos is usually prepared at least in part by financial public relations specialists. Value Line reports as well as individual Standard & Poor's "tear sheets" indicate the availability of a DRP plan and supply the phone number of the company. Another excellent source is Standard & Poor's Directory of Dividend Reinvestment Plans, issued each spring and fall. This paperback volume lists key plan features and provides company addresses and shareholder-information phone numbers. A useful newsletter called *The Moneypaper* (the phone number is (914) 381-5400 informs subscribers of details on DRPs, allowing the investor to make initial purchases directly from the companies.

DISADVANTAGES OF DRPs FOR THE INVESTOR

- Inability to impose price limits on orders to buy or sell the shares through the plan.

- Inability to time purchases as desired, as for tax planning or in case of news events.

- When liquidating a position, the need to place two orders (one with a broker and a second with the DRP) since two lots of shares are held (sometimes can be overcome if the DRP will accept deposits of share certificates).

- Nearly always requires investor to take physical delivery of stock certificate he or she might otherwise leave in brokerage account ("street name"). However, many plans then allow the participant to voluntarily deposit certificates (if identically registered) into the plan for safekeeping.

- Although some utilities have begun to make provisions for retirement plans (IRAs and Keoghs), in most cases it is impossible to participate in a DRP within the custodianship structure of a qualified retirement plan.

The latter point is perhaps the most unfortunate, since the features of a DRP and an IRA are so well matched: automatic compounding within a tax-deferred account, systematic investment, a steady current return from dividends, and long-term investing are positives encouraged through a DRP but only occasionally possible in a DRP/IRA combination. The DRP prospectus will usually indicate whether the plan allows participation by IRAs, Keogh accounts, and similar plans. If not, there is usually an "800" phone number where the question can readily be answered.

SUMMARY

The proper and currently monitored choice of utility stocks is much more critical to investment success than whether a particular stock can be used in a tax-sheltered plan. Buy and hold only on the investment merits, *not* on the ability to use an IRA plan! The opposite reasoning is the equivalent of buying an ugly or poorly made suit because it is available on sale.

The much more important and subtle dangers in dividend-reinvestment plans affect all holders, not just those interested in IRA compatibility. The first, present in all plans, is the loyalty and habit factor. When you have been doing something for some time on a periodic basis—like letting dividends be reinvested, and/or adding cash voluntarily—it is psychologically difficult to reverse field and sell the stock. Earlier chapters have demonstrated that there is indeed a time to sell utility stocks and have shown how to identify those times. It is important not to allow membership in the DRP, despite the historically provided benefits, to deter the sell decision. At most, one might leave a tiny balance in the account (perhaps five or fewer shares) to allow a later purchase decision to be executed at low or zero brokerage cost.

The second subtle danger that DRPs pose is the lure of a bargain. Low- or zero-cost reinvesting and cash investing options are attractive, and the ability to buy more shares at a discount is really attractive. Unless the company's fortunes are decaying! Then the minimal amount of discount price makes the plan seem worth joining but in fact will prove a poor reason for investing. The investor should buy a utility (or any other kind of) stock on its own merits, not because a discount-DRP is available. Use the same common sense as in a department store or supermarket: bad merchandise on sale is not really a bargain.

For those readers interested in the DRP availability of utilities whose stocks they are already considering, this chapter concludes with a listing of such plans as of late 1992. Naturally, this source will become less useful over the years, so investors should contact the companies or use the sources cited above for current information.

Utility Dividend Reinvestment Plans without Discounts

WATER
 CALIF. WATER SRVC
 CONSUMERS WATER
 IWC RESOURCES
 MIDDLESEX WATER
 SOUTHERN CALIF. WTR

GAS

ARKLA INC.
ATLANTA GAS LIGHT
ATMOS ENERGY
BERKSHIRE GAS CO.
BROOKLYN UNION GAS
CASCADE NAT GAS
CONN. ENERGY
CONN. NAT GAS
CONSOL. NAT GAS
DELTA NATURAL GAS
EASTERN ENTS.
ENERGEN CORP.
ENRON CORP.
ENSERCH CORP
EQUITABLE RESOURCES
INDIANA ENERGY
INTERPROVINCIAL PPL
KN ENERGY, INC.
LACLEDE GAS

MAPCO, INC.
MCN CORP.
MOBILE GAS SVC
N.J. RESOURCES
NATIONAL FUEL GAS
NICOR INC.
NORTHWEST NATURAL GAS
ONEOK INC.
PEOPLES ENERGY
PROVIDENCE ENGY
QUESTAR CORP.
SO'EASTN MICH. GAS
SONAT INC
SOUTHW'N ENERGY
SOUTHWEST GAS
TENNECO, INC.
WASHINGTON GAS LT
WICOR, INC
WILLIAMS COS.
WISC. SOUTHERN GAS

PHONE

ALLTEL CORP.
AMER. TEL & TEL
AMERITECH CORP.
BELL ATLANTIC
BELLSOUTH CORP.
CENTEL CORP.
CENTURY TEL.
CINCINNATI BELL
COMM. SATELLITE

GTE CORP.
LINCOLN TELECOM
NYNEX CORP.
PACIFIC TELESIS
ROCHESTER TEL.
SOUTHERN N.E. TEL
SOUTHW'N BELL
SPRINT CORP.
U S WEST INC.

ELECTRIC

ALLEGHENY POWER
AMER. ELEC PWR
ATLANTIC ENERGY
BANGOR HYDRO-ELEC
BLACK HILLS CORP.
BOSTON EDISON
CAROLINA PWR & LT
CEN. LA. ELEC.
CEN. VT. P.S.
CENTERIOR ENGY
CENTRAL & SW
CILCORP INC.
CMS ENERGY CORP
CMNWTH ENERGY

KU ENERGY CORP.
LONG ISL. LIGHT.
MDU RESOURCES
MIDWEST RES'S
MINNESOTA P&L
MONTANA POWER
N'THW'N PUB SRV
NEVADA POWER
NEW ENG. ELEC.
NIAGARA MOHAWK
NIPSCO INDS.
NORTHEAST UTIL
NRTHN STS POWER
OHIO EDISON
ORANGE & ROCKLD

CONSOL. EDISON
DELMARVA POWER
DETROIT EDISON
DOMINION RESRCS
DPL INC.
DQE
DUKE POWER
ENTERGY CORP.
FLORIDA PROGRESS
FPL GROUP
GEN'L PUB UTIL
HAWAIIAN ELEC.
HOUSTON INDS.
IDAHO POWER
IES INDUSTRIES
ILLINOIS POWER
INTERSTATE PWR
IOWA-ILL GAS & EL
IPALCO ENTERP.
KANSAS PWR & LT

OTTER TAIL PWR
PENN. PWR & LIGHT
PHILA. ELECTRIC
PORTLAND GEN'L
POTOMAC ELECTR.
PSI RESOURCES
PUBLIC SVC ENT.
PUGET SOUND P&L
SCANA CORP.
SCECORP
SIERRA PACIFIC
SOUTHERN CO.
SOUTHW'N PUB SV
TECO ENERGY
TNP ENTERPRISES
UNION ELECTRIC
UNITED ILLUMINATING
UPPER PENINSULA EN
WASHINGTON W.P.
WISC. ENERGY
WPL HOLDINGS

GAS & ELECTRIC

BALTIMORE G&E
CEN. HUDSON G&E
CINCINNATI G&E
CIPSCO INC.
CMNWTH EDISON
LG&E ENERGY
MADISON GAS & EL

N.Y. STATE E&G
NORTHW'N PUB SVC
OKLAHOMA GAS & EL
PACIFIC G & E
ROCHESTER G&E
SAN DIEGO G & E
SOUTH'N IND G&E
ST. JOE LT & PWR

DIVERSIFIED

BCE INC.
CHESAPEAKE UTILS
CITIZENS UTILITIES
FLA. PUBLIC UTILS
PACIFICORP

Utility Dividend Reinvestment Plans with Discounts

COMPANY NAME	PERCENT DISCOUNT
WATER	
AMER. WATER WKS	5
CONN. WATER SVC	5
E'TOWN CORP.	5
PHILA. SUBURBAN	5
SOUTHWEST WATER	5
UNITED WATER	5
GAS	
BAY STATE GAS	2
COLONIAL GAS	5
ENERGYNORTH	5
NORTH CAROLINA GAS	5
NUI CORP.	5
PANHANDLE EASTERN	5
PIEDMONT NAT GAS	5
PUBLIC SVC (N.C.)	5
SOUTH JERSEY IND.	3
UGI CORP.	5
UNITED CITIES GAS	5
VALLEY RESOURCES	5
WASHINGTON ENERGY	5
WESTCOAST ENERGY	5
PHONE	
TELEPHONE & DATA	5
ELECTRIC	
CEN. MAINE PWR	5
EASTERN UTILITIES	5
EMPIRE DISTRICT EL.	5
GREEN MTN. PWR.	5
SOUTHW'N ELECTRIC	5
TEXAS UTILITIES	5
UNITIL CORP.	5
GAS & ELECTRIC	
PUBLIC SVC COLO.	3
DIVERSIFIED	
UTILICORP UNITED	5

TWENTY-FIVE

Using Utility Mutual Funds and Closed-End Funds

Having learned the important considerations and action signals for success in utilities investing, the individual investor may sense a lack of time for doing the necessary research and tracking. There are, after all, over 200 public utility common stocks in the United States alone. Or, with the experience of recent years still fresh in memory, the individual may be acutely aware of institutional dominance in the marketplace. And, unless the reader is already comfortably wealthy, there may be a well-grounded fear of lack of diversification. The mutual fund approach to investment offers attractions that respond to these concerns. With a mutual fund, one acquires professional management and the research acumen and time to cover all the available companies; one becomes part of the institutional action rather than a possible victim of it; and one gains wide diversification.

ADVANTAGES OF USING FUNDS

So, the sharp reader might ask, why bother to do it for oneself; why not just buy a good utilities fund? These questions are especially pertinent when some of the other advantages of funds are considered:

- Some are no-load funds, allowing purchase without commissions.

- One can invest small amounts periodically or occasionally without suffering the high commission rates of small stock transactions.

- Similarly, one may easily withdraw any dollar amount either regularly (as for monthly living expenses) or when specific sums are needed.

- Dividends can be automatically reinvested by the fund if the investor so desires.

- Mutual fund purchases and sales are not subject to possible adverse executions due to intra-day fluctuations, as are individual stocks.

- A special breed of investment company, known as the closed-end fund, can sometimes be bought at a discount to its inherent asset value, affording higher income and greater chance for appreciation.

- Reinvestment of closed-end funds' dividends can sometimes be done at discounts to market value, raising total return.

- Some funds can invest internationally, affording the investor exposure to economies in other nations that would be difficult to research personally.

Some of the above aspects of funds have virtue, to be sure. But these advantages should not induce the investor to assume that just any utilities fund will be ideal for the job. Just as some individual stocks in a generally attractive industry will prove better than others, there are significant differences among utilities funds.

COSTS OF INVESTING VIA FUNDS

A utilities fund, like any mutual fund, unit trust, or limited partnership, is essentially a manufactured financial product. It has been created to meet a known need among investors. The fund management company receives a fee, *averaging around 0.65% per annum,* based on the total assets under management in the fund. The fund itself bears other nonadvisory expenses such as legal and auditing fees, commissions, and custodian and transfer agent expenses, among others. These on average bring the total expense ratio to about 1.25%. And funds that have front-end commissions and/or back-end exit charges are sold by professional salespeople. A dollar of commissions paid is a dollar not invested for the prior owner's lifetime.

DISADVANTAGES OF INVESTING IN UTILITIES FUNDS

The previous section alluded to the palpable costs of investing via funds. Sometimes those costs are less than the individual would incur to invest in a portfolio of stocks directly; sometimes they are more. But there are other and probably more critical issues to be weighed in considering investing in utilities via funds. These are more subtle, but they are directly related to the principles for successful investment developed earlier in this book. Some funds pass muster and others seem to fall short when examined on this basis.

A mutual fund, being an investment product, must have features that will attract buyers to put their dollars into it. If it is a fund sold via commissioned salespeople (brokers, or company fund salespeople), it must have features that make it attractive to sell. The utilities mutual fund competes fairly directly for the investor's dollar with individual utility stocks—as well as with bond funds, CDs, and government and municipal bonds. The salesperson and the individual investor make the choices of what is bought. Since utilities investors are concerned with yield, the fund's ability to offer an attractive current return (read, "the highest yield") is therefore a major selling point to both the broker and the investor. That is where the problem arises.

As has been demonstrated earlier in the book, being among the highest yielders among utility stocks is a sign of risk and an indicator of likely low (rather than high) total return. The highest yields are associated with lack of growth in the income stream. But to overcome the burden of its own advisory fee and other expenses, a fund is naturally drawn in the direction of loading its portfolio with stocks providing well-above-average current yields. If, for example, natural gas stocks generally yield about 6%, and a fund's total expense ratio is typically 1.25%, the natural gas stock fund manager must achieve a gross return of 7.25% on invested assets to compete on even ground for the investor's dollar. The sophisticated investor may pay something for diversification plus the other benefits listed earlier, but current yield is usually the biggest and brightest lure to the broker and investor.

One better way in which a fund manager can achieve an attractive current yield and at the same time reduce the risk of capital loss is to place part of the fund into utility bonds rather than hold all assets in stocks. This mix, in the long run, may well produce a satisfactory current cash return without taking the risks to capital that come with looking for the highest current yields available among utility *common* stocks alone. Duff & Phelps Utilities Income, Inc., a closed-end fund traded on the NYSE, has used this approach to both enhance gross current return and reduce risk of capital loss. The fund's stated objectives are both current and growing income. For the investor willing to forego some current income, however, the mixed-portfolio type of fund may not be the first choice. No fund, utility or otherwise, can be right for everyone—any more than a single stock can be right for all. More than one approach can work.

Another significant burden that a utilities fund manager can face is the implications of the fund's own size. While diversification has its benefits, size becomes a detriment at some point. As a fund—utility or otherwise—becomes extremely large (say, for example, over $1 billion in assets) it must either lengthen its list of holdings, or focus only on the larger-capitalization issues in which it can take major positions. Lengthening the list of holdings requires added research staff time and necessarily moves the fund, on average, further down the list from the manager's true top choices. Focusing on large-cap stocks implies restricting much of the portfolio to the mature, big-name utilities that typically represent the slower-growing industrial states and cities. The implication: lack of dividend growth.

If a billion dollar fund owns a list of 100 companies (further down the list of available pickings than the author would like to go!), the average position will be $10 million. If a utility stock trades at $20 per share, that means a 500,000-share block per position. Such blocks are not easy to trade (in or out) in some of the more attractive, faster-growth utilities. Size becomes its own trap. Funds widely publicized in the press for recent success, funds heavily advertised by well-known major sponsors, and house-brand funds of the major brokerage firms are prone to the dangers of becoming too big. They generally would not be the author's first choices.

Mutual funds (and not alone those specializing in utility stocks) also suffer the effects of adverse money flows because of investors' shifts in preferences. At the top of any market, and this includes even nonspeculative market cycles such as those in long-term interest rates, investors and brokers tend to jump on the bandwagon. From the fund manager's point of view, this means cash is pouring into the fund when the manager, deep in his or her own heart, would rather not buy anything more.

But it is especially true of sector funds that they are expected to remain virtually fully invested in their chosen field rather than try to time the market. So, at the top the utilities fund manager is impelled to buy stocks well down the list of attractiveness, or to load up on favorite names already fully priced, just to keep the cash percentage in the fund suitably low. At or near market bottoms, fund shareholders panic and redeem shares, thereby forcing portfolio liquidations at just the wrong time and hurting those shareholders who remain invested.

CLOSED-END FUNDS' ADVANTAGES

Closed-end funds, by contrast, are essentially closed pools of money and therefore do not suffer the cash-flow adversity felt by their open-end cousins. This is one of their virtues. In the case of closed-end funds, however, the public must be cautious about any upswing in the number of new offerings and/or rights offerings; the easy ability of the underwriters to bring such new product to market often implies an already overly enthusiastic (read, "over-bought") market. Timing in buying a closed-end fund is thus a critical element for success: be cautious if the price premium vs. the fund's NAV has already been rising or the discount narrowing for a long period.

THE BOTTOM LINE: CAREFUL SELECTION FOR TOTAL RETURN

The reader should be not at all surprised to find that the implication for selecting a utilities fund is just the opposite of what the broker will most commonly try to sell: yields well above the average should be a warning of likely low *total* return. Therefore, the funds most likely to provide inherent fund benefits while not mixing in the drawbacks discussed above are those whose specific investment policies are aimed at total return, including growth of capital. How can the investor separate such funds from the pack? There are three principal ways:

- First, read the language in the prospectus, under "investment policies and practices," very carefully. Avoid funds that emphasize "high" or "maximum" current cash return. Seek those that speak of "growth in income and capital" and in particular those that specifically refer to requiring growing dividends for a stock to be bought or held.

- Second, do not settle for a prospectus alone. Insist on having the latest annual or semi-annual report. Incredibly in this age of consumer protection, the prospectus legally need not contain the list of portfolio holdings. These must appear in the semi- and annual reports. The astute funds investor must examine them. The stocks being held should include those you would buy or hold by using the dividend-signal rules developed in this book. If the list contains more than a sprinkling of nongrowers, expect the fund's high current yield to be offset by periodic setbacks in net asset value (NAV) per share as the highest-yielding stocks cut or omit their dividends. You can do better than that on your own. A small, but only a small, group of current nongrowers is permissible within the list.

On occasion a really good portfolio manager or team will validly identify a once-troubled issue that in their best judgment will weather its storm and begin raising dividends again. An example is Detroit Edison in 1990. But if a DTE were to be accompanied by numerous very-high-yield names such as Centerior, Commonwealth, Nevada Power, Ohio Edison, Arkla, Transco, and Pacific Enterprises one could perhaps assume that Detroit Edison was a fortunate rather than an astute choice. The others, being very high yielders, were poised for falls. So select only funds whose actual portfolio lists primarily follow the rules for success, not those that reach for highest current yield.

- Finally, look for those funds which have actually compiled the most successful records. Compare the "mountain charts" inside the prospectuses. Look for the funds whose tables of total return (not cash return) show the higher numbers over five- or ten-year periods. Inevitably, these are the funds whose managers have invested for total return including capital appreciation, rather than those that have sought maximum current yield.

Following, courtesy of Lipper Analytical Services, Inc., is a list of mutual funds and closed-end funds concentrating on utilities and having at least $100 million in total assets as of early 1993 (Table 25.1). Comparative total return, rather than highest current yield, should be the investor's primary selection criterion. Read the current prospectus and annual or semi-annual report before investing in any mutual fund.

TABLE 25.1 Five-Year and One-Year Total Returns (Percent) and Ranks of Funds with 1992 Assets over $100 Million

Fund Name	Fund size 09/30/92 (Mill $)	Total Returns (Percent) and Ranks		1 year to 12/31/92		1 year to 12/31/91		1 year to 12/31/90		1year to 12/31/89		1 year to 12/31/88	
		5 years 12/31/92											
Fidelity Sel Util.	259	117.9	1	10.6	5	21.0	13	0.6	7	39.0	1	16.5	2
Prudential Utility;B	3262	104.3	2	9.0	13	19.0	15	-6.5	15	37.2	2	22.8	1
Duff & Phelps Util Income:CEF	1414	100.8	3	10.0	8	25.8	4	2.7	3	26.3	8	11.8	10
Liberty Util Fund	578	99.2	4	9.1	11	25.8	4	2.0	4	23.6	13	15.1	4
Fortress Utility	363	98.5	5	8.9	14	25.9	3	0.9	6	26.1	9	13.8	8
Fidelity Util Income	881	97.8	6	10.9	3	21.2	12	1.9	5	25.9	10	14.8	5
Eaton Vance Total Return	563	97.1	7	6.6	21	23.6	8	0.2	9	33.5	5	11.9	9
Colonial Utilities; A	201	94.0	8	21.0	1	25.9	2	-5.1	13	17.8	15	13.9	7
Financial Port: Utilities	106	91.6	9	10.8	4	27.9	1	-10.0	16	31.5	6	14.2	6
Franklin Cust: Utilities	2191	91.0	10	9.1	12	24.2	6	0.4	8	25.9	11	11.7	11
ABT Util income FD	142	89.5	11	10.4	6	17.9	17	-6.1	14	34.1	4	15.6	3
AIM: Utilities(C)	105	106.24	*	7.9	17	23.7	7	-3.0	12	36.1	3	#	#
Dean Witter Utilities	2690	73.25	*	8.8	15	18.9	16	-0.3	10	24.5	12	#	#
Global Utility Fund; A	115	35.30	*	9.3	10	22.4	9	9.5	1	-7.58#	#	*	*
IDS Utilities Income	459	80.15	*	11.3	2	22.0	10	-1.7	11	28.6	7	#	#
Liberty Finl: Utilities	107	15.85	*	10.4	7	4.97#	#	*	*	*	*	*	*
Merrill Glbl Utility; B	184	23.20	*	8.1	16	14.0	20	0.00#	#	*	*	*	*
Prudential Utility; A	175	29.79	*	9.9	9	20.0	14	-1.53#	#	*	*	*	*
Putnam Util Gr & Inc; A	415	28.05	*	7.2	20	14.4	19	4.47#	#	*	*	*	*
Shearson Inc: Util; B	1936	73.92	*	7.2	19	21.8	11	3.3	2	20.6	14	#	#
SM Barney: Utility; A	124	26.13	*	7.5	18	17.3	18	0.08#	#	*	*	*	*
Vanguard Spl: Utilities	225	12.16	#	12.16	#	*	*	*	*	*	*	*	*
Averages and Fund Counts	755	98.3	11	9.7	21	21.6	20	-0.7	16	28.7	15	14.7	11

Notes: CEF: Closed-End Fund   SOURCE: Lipper Analytical Services, Inc.
*–Fund not in operation for full period; result shown is for life of fund
#-Fund first offered in this year; result shown is since inception

TAX CONSIDERATIONS

Ironically, there is one other aspect of investing via funds that may be a potential problem for the taxable investor in the otherwise-best funds. A good (capital-gain-achieving) utilities fund is more likely than a maximum-cash-return oriented fund to have unrealized gains on the books. These can be found on the balance sheet, where total cost is compared with total present market value of the portfolio holdings. In buying a fund with significant embedded unrealized gains, the investor is acquiring a potential tax liability, one over whose timing he or she has no control. For example, suppose a $20 mutual fund contains $3 per share of unrealized capital gains. When these are cashed in, about $1 per share of tax will be due from the investor. Thus the $20 is worth $19 after taxes if the portfolio manager should decide to take all the gains. The same problem can apply among closed-end funds. However, several academic studies have demonstrated that closed-end funds' shares tend to trade in the market at prices that reflect, at least partly, embedded capital gains tax liabilities. Solutions to the tax problem are as follows:

- Buy closed-end utilities funds at discounts to NAV if at all possible; if the fund typically sells at a premium, try to time purchases at the lower end of the historic band of premiums;

- Buy open-end mutual funds when interest rates are up rather than down, thus implying smaller embedded capital gains included in the purchase price; and

- Buy and hold funds in nontaxable accounts (IRAs, Keoghs, 401(k) or 403(b) plans) or in children's accounts where the marginal tax bracket can be lower than for the employed adult.

CONCLUSION

The bottom line on investing in utilities via funds is a mixed verdict. Not all funds will provide the type of result the educated utility investor should insist upon receiving. The more attractive funds are those seeking total return through *growth* of capital and the income stream, rather than maximum current cash income. In practice, due to the pressures of competing yields and the lure of the high current return, such funds will be in the minority. If you truly need maximum current cash flow, consider buying the growing-income fund and setting up automatic monthly or quarterly withdrawals that exceed actual income earned. That way, not all of what you spend will be taxable income, and you will sidestep the capital risks involved in chasing the highest yielders.

One other aspect of funds may be useful: because the fund is typically widely diversified, the performance of a utility fund over time may be a better benchmark measure than one of the popular utility average (e.g., the Dow Jones 15 Utility Average). But be sure to look for total returns rather than change in net asset value, since funds must pay out their net realized capital gains annually and each distribution reduces net asset value by an equal amount.

TWENTY-SIX

One of the major objections raised against investing in utilities is the burden of current taxation on the income stream. For individual investors in the prime earning years, when income is taxed at the maximum bracket, this is a very real concern. The drag of income taxes is also one of the major reasons cited for centering an investment program around growth rather than around current income. The initial Clinton tax proposals favored capital gains over regular income, thus enhancing the argument for emphasis in this direction.

This chapter addresses antidotes—one hesitates to use the word "cures"—for the tax problem in utility investing. Careful planning can provide significant buffers against taxes and can allow the investor to exert some control over the timing of tax events.

TOTAL-RETURN INVESTING: THE NATURAL SHIELD

Earlier chapters have dealt with the importance of avoiding highest current return as the primary means of utilities investing. The much greater rewards and significantly lower risks of a total-return approach have been demonstrated. Following this approach provides the individual investor with a natural (albeit partial) tax shield. The greater the portion of overall return that is generated in the form of current cash dividend returns, the higher will be the effective tax rate on the overall return. Conversely, the larger the portion of total return that is generated by capital growth, the lower the effective tax rate on the overall return—and the more the investor will have control over the timing of tax payments.

The following example illustrates the different tax burdens that result from current-return versus total-return investing in utilities. Current dividend yield levels will vary considerably with the overall interest-rate climate, as they have in the past (see Chapter 18). Thus the following illustration is applicable as a general guide although the details will be different in future years.

Assume: Federal marginal income tax rate of 28%.

State marginal income tax rate of 5%.

(For simplicity, ignore cross deductions for taxes.)

Current dividend yield on zero-growth utility is 9%.

Current dividend yield on high-growth utility is 7.5%.

Dividend growth rate for high-growth utility is 4.5%.

Prevailing interest rates remain unchanged.

Overview: Expected total returns *before taxes* are as follows:

High-Yield Utility with Zero Growth	High-Growth Utility with Lower Yield
9.0% cash	7.5% cash
0.0 capital	4.5 capital
9.0% total	12.0% total
higher risk to capital	lower risk to capital

Tax Benefit: Because only the current (cash) return is taxable in the year of receipt, the relative advantage of the total-return investing strategy is even greater on an after-tax basis. This is because *returns on an after-tax basis* are as follows:

High-Yield Utility with Zero Growth	High-Growth Utility with Lower Yield
9.0% cash	7.5% cash
-3.0 taxes at 33%	-2.5 taxes at 33%
0.0 capital	4.5 capital
6.0% after current taxes	9.5% after current taxes

Thus the relative gross-yield advantage of 33 percent (12% return for the total-return approach versus just 9% for the high-current-yield approach) shifts up to nearly 60% (9.5% vs. 6%) on an after-tax basis. It is true that taxes will eventually need to be paid. But the advantages of deferring the taxes are considerable:

- Some degree of control over timing
- Ability to earn returns on the tax dollars until those dollars actually are paid
- Possibilities for reducing or totally avoiding tax later

The potentials for reducing the tax burden or avoiding it are only partly within the investor's control; a great deal is determined by the external environment. The major variable is the level of taxes on capital gains and the ability to control how and when that tax is actually paid.

As this book was written, the shift from the Bush to the Clinton presidency implied little to no near-term likelihood of an across-the-board or indiscriminate reduction in the federal tax on capital gains. Perhaps the next shift of the political or ideological pendulum may generate such a change back toward the earlier model in which capital gains are taxed at a significantly lower rate. Such a window in time would provide an opportune point for investors to nail down capital gains rather than expose them to potentially higher rates at some future point.

But one major control element that an investor has in shielding capital gains from taxation, or at least lowering the burden, lies in timing. While there is no way to avoid timing current taxation on dividend income, major capital gains may be timed for realization in years when any of the following occur:

- Retirement, decreasing income level to lower marginal bracket
- Age 65, providing the shelter of larger personal exemptions
- A work sabbatical or career change or job interruption, any of which might lower one year's marginal tax bracket

- Voluntary gifting of the assets to a child or grandchild or aged parent, who sells the asset (realizing the same overall gain from your low basis, but probably being taxed at a lower or zero bracket)

- Other capital losses available to offset the gain fully or in part

LEGAL TAX SHIELDS: NOT NATURAL, BUT VERY USEFUL

While the difference between total-return investing and current-income investing carries its own natural difference (advantages) in current-year tax burden, several features of the U.S. tax code provide opportunities for investing in utilities in ways that can postpone all current taxation on dividends earned. These are as follows:

- Individual Retirement Arrangements ("IRAs")
- Employer-Sponsored 401(k) and 403(b) Plans
- Keogh Plans (for the self-employed)
- Investing via Variable Annuity and/or Variable Life Insurance Contracts
- Holding assets in a child's name

The IRA, although in recent years unfortunately no longer contribution-deductible for most taxpayers, still represents an outstanding opportunity to build retirement assets free of current taxation on the increase. Even if the contribution cannot be deducted from current-year taxable income, both the income stream on the assets and any capital gains realized within the IRA account are 100% shielded from taxation until withdrawals begin. The IRA vehicle, because it starts at a small size, might well be invested early in a mutual fund specializing in utility stocks (subject to caveats and qualifications noted in the prior chapter!). Later, after some critical mass has developed, the investor might shift the IRA to a self-managed brokerage account and select individual utility stocks according to the principles revealed in this book—and perhaps step aside into a money-market fund during periods of rising interest rates, which a mutual fund will not do.

Employer-sponsored plans provide sheltering of gains similar to that available under an IRA. Not all employers offer such plans. Some who do have them will match or partially match employee contributions. This feature represents a very high return on the investor's saved dollars. It should be taken advantage of to the greatest extent possible. A typical 401(k) plan—for employees in the private sector—allows up to a certain percentage of wage or salary income to be diverted from the current income stream into the investment plan. There is no federal or state income taxation on the contribution before it goes in. Such plans are often referred to with titles such as "voluntary salary-reduction and savings plans." Similar arrangements are available as 403(b) plans for public-sector employees such as teachers, and for employees of nonprofits. The 401(k) and 403(b) plans allow putting aside and sheltering from tax on future income more than the $2,000 annual IRA contribution. But many 401(k) and 403(b) plans offer relatively limited investment choices. Typically there is a money-market-type option, plus a bond-fund option, and often a common-stock-fund option. In the case of a publicly traded company, often there is an option to buy shares in the employer. Not very commonly does one find a plan with so many investment options as to include specifically a utility-stock fund—especially one investing on total-return principles!

Keogh plans, popularly named after Eugene Keogh, the U.S. Congressman from New York who sponsored the 1962 legislation creating them, are like IRAs in many ways—but with some key differences. Keoghs are available only to persons with self-employment income. The maximum annual contribution is a percentage of self-employment income rather than a flat $2,000. And the self-employed person (for example a doctor or shop-keeper) who has any employee(s) (such as a nurse or clerk) must make contributions to those employees' accounts in the same percentage of their incomes as on his or her own income. The tax-deferral benefits of asset build-up inside a Keogh are the same as those for an IRA. Thus the earlier comments on how to use IRAs advantageously for investing in utility stocks apply equally to a Keogh account.

Another, less well publicized but increasingly popular, tax shield is the Variable Annuity or Variable Life Insurance contract. As of December 31, 1992, some $79.3 billion of assets were in such places. While a fixed annuity and a conventional whole-life policy provide a guaranteed result (contractually promised monthly income level or minimum cash value), the variable products shift some of the risk and potential reward to the individual. An insurance company invests premium dollars or annuity sums in various media such as real estate, stocks, and bonds. In a fixed life or annuity contract the company takes the risk that its investment results will exceed its promised obligations to the policy owner.

In variable products, the owner directs the investments within the contract's legal and tax umbrella; the owner realizes the results of these investment decisions, for better or worse, when the eventual payouts are made. If the investments have been highly successful, the annuity stream or the cash value will be higher than under a fixed contract. The contract is a legal wrapper around a specialized group of mutual funds or "separate accounts" among which the contract owner may choose, and switch from time to time. At the end of 1992, about 76% of such assets were invested in equities.

In some cases a utility fund is one of the investment options available. Provided this fund is managed with total return rather than current income as the primary goal, it can be a good investment choice. All the inside buildup of income and capital gains occurs with taxes deferred until the policyholder takes distributions. Thus the tax-deferral feature is very much like that occurring within an IRA or Keogh or 401(k) account. The major relative positive feature of the variable contracts is the unlimited amount of assets that can be placed into them for shelter. The major negative is the often-high level of sales charges, annual fees, and management expenses of the investment funds—as well as escape penalties for up to the first seven years after the contract is bought. These should be considered carefully before entering such contracts.

Building up assets through utility investing in the name and Social Security Account Number of a child is another way to achieve some tax shelter. I sent one of my two children to college almost entirely on savings amassed in this manner. However, in recent years the U.S. tax code has restricted this route: as of 1992 only $1,200 per year of investment income received in the name of a child under age 14 could be taxed at the low 15% marginal bracket; the rest was constructively taxed at the parent's marginal bracket.

Nevertheless, this shield is of some value and should not be overlooked. A college fund of $20,000 earning current income at 6% would have all its dividend stream taxed in the lower bracket. The capital gains from well-chosen growth utilities could be timed to be realized before the child's tax bracket rises, and in time to pay for college costs. And the capital gains are taxed at the child's marginal rate, not the parent's. (Similar low-bracket benefits apply to income earned in the name of an aged person with no employment income and perhaps little or no taxable pension; here the under-14 rule does not apply, making the tax strategy even more attractive. Supporting a parent can cost less if the income used for their benefit is earned and taxed in their name at a presumably lower bracket than yours.) In all cases, of course, transfers of assets should be carefully planned so as to avoid or minimize gift taxes.

Readers are cautioned that the tax laws change and the specific circumstances of individual taxpayers may make tax approaches described above inapplicable or of questionable value when considered in an overall planning context. The purpose of this book is not to offer tax advice, which should be received from qualified professionals. The purpose of this chapter has been to point out the existence of several potentially worthwhile avenues of tax deferral and/or reduction that existed at the time of writing and publication. This should serve as a starting point in the future tax thinking of the individual reader who should explore tax-related opportunities and risks as they currently exist.

Tax considerations should seldom, if ever, be the governing factor in an investment decision; in fact, the necessity to pay taxes on gains is often used as a faulty rationalization for not selling investments that really should be closed out. But where there are tax-advantaged ways to structure or hold income-producing investments—such as utility stocks—they should be carefully considered rather than ignored.

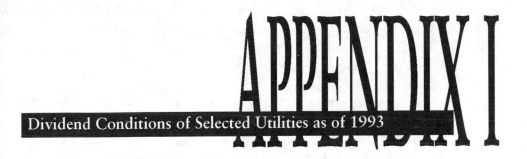

Dividend Conditions of Selected Utilities as of 1993

The primary purpose of this book is to educate the utilities investor in a system for monitoring companies' dividend growth patterns as a means of generating buy/hold/avoid/sell signals. Chapters 14 and 15 described and explained this system in detail. While the primary value of this book will be an enduring one in that it provides the owner with a method of analysis—one readily useful in the hands of the nonprofessional—inevitably the earliest readers will ask, "what are the companies' dividend condition signals now?" Therefore, the following tables provide a snapshot of dividend conditions as of February 1993.

As a convenient reference, following are the six dividend condition signals introduced earlier in the book:

CONDITION 1: STEADY GROWTH

CONDITION 2: DECELERATING GROWTH

CONDITION 3: PRIOR GROWTH, NOW ZERO GROWTH

CONDITION 4: REDUCTION

CONDITION 5: OMISSION

CONDITION 6: ACCELERATION OR RESTORATION

The reader is strongly cautioned to track subsequent dividend patterns up to the time of purchase or holding of each stock, rather than to rely on the companies' history through only early 1993. Signals change, and with them the implied investment actions!

	Ticker Symbol	12/92 Div Rt	Percent Div GR 92 vs.91	January 1993 Dividend Condition

CONDITION 1: STEADY GROWTH

Company	Ticker Symbol	12/92 Div Rt	Percent Div GR 92 vs.91	January 1993 Dividend Condition
ALLTEL CORP.	AT	1.60	8.0	1
ATLANTIC ENERGY	ATE	1.52	1.3	1
ATMOS ENERGY	ATO	1.28	3.1	1
BALTIMORE G&E	BGE	1.44	2.9	1
BAY STATE GAS	BGC	1.38	3.0	1
BELL ATLANTIC	BEL	2.60	3.2	1
BRITISH TELECOM	BTY	3.39	5.9	1
BROOKLYN UNION	BU	1.98	2.1	1
CALIF. WATER	CWTR	1.86	3.3	1
CAROLINA POWER	CPL	3.28	3.8	1
CASCADE NAT GAS	CGC	1.40	2.9	1
CEN. HUDSON G&E	CNH	2.00	4.2	1
CEN. LA. ELEC.	CNL	1.38	3.0	1
CENTURY TEL.	CTL	0.44	3.5	1
CIPSCO INC.	CIP	1.92	2.1	1
CONN. NAT GAS	CTG	1.44	0.2	1
CONSOL. NAT GAS	CNG	1.92	1.1	1
DETROIT EDISON	DTE	1.98	5.3	1
DOMINION RESRCS	D	2.46	3.7	1
DQE	DQE	1.60	5.3	1
DUKE POWER	DUK	1.80	4.7	1
EMPIRE DIST EL	EDE	1.28	2.4	1
FLA. PROGRESS	FPC	1.94	2.5	1
FPL GROUP	FPL	2.44	1.7	1
GREEN MTN. PWR.	GMP	2.10	1.9	1
GTE CORP.	GTE	1.82	7.1	1
INDIANA ENERGY	IEI	1.48	4.2	1
INTERSTATE PWR	IPW	2.08	2.0	1
IPALCO ENTERP.	IPL	1.96	4.3	1
KANSAS CITY P&L	KLT	1.44	2.9	1
KU ENERGY CORP.	KU	1.56	4.0	1
LG&E ENERGY	LGE	2.01	3.3	1
MCN CORP.	MCN	1.68	2.4	1
MONTANA POWER	MTP	1.58	2.6	1
N.Y. STATE E&G	NGE	2.16	1.9	1
NICOR INC.	GAS	2.36	5.4	1

NRTHN STS POWER	NSP	2.52	4.1	1
NW NATURAL GAS	NWNG	1.72	0.0	1
NWN PUB SERVICE	NPS	1.62	3.6	1
ORANGE & ROCKLD	ORU	2.46	2.5	1
OTTER TAIL PWR	OTTR	1.64	2.5	1
PACIFIC G & E	PCG	1.76	7.3	1
PACIFICORP	PPW	1.54	2.7	1
PENN. PWR&LIGHT	PPL	1.60	3.2	1
PEOPLES ENERGY	PGL	1.76	2.3	1
PHILA. SUBURBAN	PSC	1.04	4.0	1
PIEDMONT NAT GS	PNY	1.84	4.5	1
QUESTAR CORP.	STR	1.06	3.9	1
ROCHESTER TEL.	RTC	1.58	2.5	1
SCANA CORP.	SCG	2.68	2.3	1
SCECORP	SCE	2.80	2.9	1
SOUTH'N IND G&E	SIG	1.56	4.0	1
SOUTHW'N ENERGY	SWN	0.60	7.1	1
TECO ENERGY	TE	1.82	5.8	1
TEXAS UTILITIES	TXU	3.04	1.3	1
UGI CORP.	UGI	1.30	4.8	1
UNION ELECTRIC	UEP	2.32	3.6	1
UNITED ILLUMIN	UIL	2.56	4.9	1
UTILICORP UNTD.	UCU	1.60	0.3	1
VALERO ENERGY	VLO	0.44	23.2	1
WASHINGTON GAS	WGL	2.14	1.9	1
WICOR, INC.	WIC	1.52	2.7	1
WISC. ENERGY	WEC	1.30	4.8	1
WISC. PUB SERV	WPS	1.74	2.4	1
WPL HOLDINGS	WPH	1.86	3.3	1

CONDITION 2: DECELERATING GROWTH

ALLEGHENY POWER	AYP	3.24	1.1	2
AMER. WATER WKS	AWK	0.92	7.0	2
ATLANTA GAS LT	ATG	2.08	2.0	2
BELLSOUTH CORP.	BLS	2.76	0.0	2
CENTEL CORP.	CNT	0.90	0.4	2
CENTRAL & SW	CSR	1.54	5.5	2
CONN. ENERGY	CNE	1.28	2.4	2
CONSOL. EDISON	ED	1.90	2.2	2
ERICSSON (ADR)	ERICY	0.60	22.4	2

GEN'L PUB UTIL	GPU	1.60	6.7	2
HAWAIIAN ELEC.	HE	2.28	1.7	2
HONG KONG TEL.	HKT	1.58	16.2	2
IOWA-ILL GAS&EL	IWG	1.73	1.2	2
KN ENERGY, INC.	KNE	1.32	6.5	2
LONG ISL. LIGHT.	LIL	1.74	2.4	2
MINNESOTA P&L	MPL	1.94	2.1	2
N'THW'N PUB SRV	NPS	1.62	2.5	2
N.J. RESOURCES	NJR	1.52	0.0	2
NAT'L FUEL GAS	NFG	1.50	2.7	2
NUI CORP.	NUI	1.58	0.0	2
NYNEX CORP.	NYN	4.64	1.8	2
PACIFIC TELESIS	PAC	2.18	1.8	2
POTOMAC ELECTR.	POM	1.60	2.6	2
ROCHESTER G&E	RGS	1.72	2.4	2
SOUTHW'N BELL	SBC	2.92	2.7	2
ST. JOE LT&PWR	SAJ	1.72	3.6	2
U S WEST INC.	USW	2.12	1.9	2
WASHINGTON ENER	WECO	1.40	0.0	2
WEST'N RESOURCES	WR	1.90	2.2	2

CONDITION 3: PRIOR GROWTH, NOW ZERO GROWTH

AMER. ELEC PWR	AEP	2.40	0.0	3
AMER. TEL & TEL	T	1.32	0.0	3
AMERITECH CORP.	AIT	3.68	4.5	3
CEN. MAINE PWR	CTP	1.56	0.0	3
CILCORP INC.	CER	2.46	0.0	3
CINCINNATI BELL	CSN	0.80	0.0	3
CINCINNATI G&E	CIN	1.65	0.0	3
CMNWTH ENERGY	CES	2.92	0.0	3
CMS ENERGY CORP	CMS	0.48	0.0	3
COASTAL CORP.	CGP	0.40	0.0	3
DELMARVA POWER	DEW	1.54	0.0	3
DPL INC.	DPL	1.08	0.0	3
EASTERN ENTS.	EFU	1.40	0.0	3
IDAHO POWER	IDA	1.86	0.0	3
IES INDUSTRIES	IES	2.10	0.0	3
ILLINOIS POWER	IPC	0.80	0.0	3
LACLEDE GAS	LG	2.40	0.0	3
MCI COM'CATIONS	MCIC	0.10	0.0	3

NEVADA POWER	NVP	1.60	0.0	3
NORTHEAST UTIL	NU	1.76	0.0	3
OKLAHOMA GAS&EL	OGE	2.66	0.0	3
PUBLIC SVC COLO	PSR	2.00	0.0	3
PUBLIC SVC ENT.	PEG	2.16	0.0	3
SOUTH JERSEY IND.	SJI	1.44	0.0	3
SOUTHN N.E. TEL	SNG	1.76	0.0	3
SOUTHW'N PUB SV	SPS	2.20	0.0	3
SPRINT CORP.	FON	1.00	0.0	3
TNP ENTERPRISES	TNP	1.63	0.0	3
UNITED WATER	UWR	0.92	0.0	3
WASHINGTON W.P.	WWP	2.48	0.0	3

CONDITION 4: REDUCTION

ARKLA INC.	ALG	0.28	-74.1	4
BURLINGTON RES.	BR	0.50	-29.1	4
CENTERIOR ENGY	CX	1.60	0.0	4
CMNWTH EDISON	CWE	1.60	-46.7	4
ENSERCH CORP.	ENS	0.20	0.0	4
MIDWEST RES'S	MWR	1.16	-25.6	4
OHIO EDISON	OEC	1.50	0.2	4
PANHANDLE EASTN	PEL	0.80	0.0	4
PORTLAND GEN'L	PGN	1.20	0.0	4
PROVIDENCE ENGY	PVY	1.00	-28.6	4
SIERRA PACIFIC	SRP	1.12	-39.1	4
SONAT INC.	SNT	0.52	-74.0	4
SOUTHWEST GAS	SWX	0.70	0.0	4
TENNECO, INC.	TGT	1.60	0.0	4
TRANSCO ENERGY	E	0.60	0.0	4

CONDITION 5: OMISSION

COLUMBIA GAS	CG	nil	N/A	5
EL PASO ELECTRC	ELPA	nil	N/A	5
GULF STS. UTIL	GSU	nil	N/A	5
PACIFIC ENTERP.	PET	nil	N/A	5
PINNACLE WEST	PNW	nil	N/A	5
PUBLIC SVC (N.M.)	PNM	nil	N/A	5
TUCSON ELEC PWR	TEP	nil	N/A	5

CONDITION 6: ACCELERATION OR RESTORATION

ALATENN RESOURCES	ATNG	1.20	9.1	6
BCE INC.	B.TO	2.56	0.0	6
BOSTON EDISON	BSE	1.70	3.7	6
CABLE & WIRELESS	CWP	0.92	5.7	6
CEN. VT. P.S.	CV	2.13	2.4	6
COMM. SATELLITE	CQ	1.40	0.0	6
EASTERN UTIL	EUA	1.44	0.0	6
ENERGEN CORP.	EGN	1.04	4.0	6
ENRON CORP.	ENE	1.40	7.7	6
ENTERGY CORP.	ETR	1.60	14.3	6
EQUITABLE RES	EQT	1.62	5.2	6
HOUSTON INDS.	HOU	3.00	1.2	6
MDU RESOURCES	MDU	1.48	2.8	6
MITCHELL ENERGY	MND	0.48	20.0	6
NEW ENGLAND ELEC.	NES	2.16	3.8	6
NIAGARA MOHAWK	NMK	0.80	25.0	6
NIPSCO INDS.	NI	1.32	6.8	6
ONEOK INC.	OKE	1.00	19.0	6
PHILA. ELECTRIC	PE	1.40	7.7	6
PSI RESOURCES	PIN	1.12	12.0	6
PUGET SOUND P&L	PSD	1.80	2.3	6
SAN DIEGO G & E	SDO	1.44	2.9	6
SOUTHERN CO.	SO	2.20	2.8	6
TELEF DE MEXICO	TMX	0.48	182.4	6
TELEFON ESPANA	TEF	1.80	11.1	6
WILLIAMS COS.	WMB	1.52	8.6	6

In compiling this listing shortly before going to press, I was struck by the strong clustering of telephone companies in the Condition 2 category and the sprinkling even in the Condition 3 grouping. This may have implications for some upward shift in the traditionally lower yields among this group, relative to others such as electric or gas companies. Also clear is the presence of a large number of gas pipeline and distribution companies in the Condition 4 and Condition 5 listings. For those looking ahead, this may imply that much of the damage to stock prices for this group had already been suffered by the end of 1992. While the population of water companies is relatively small, note that none are in Condition 6 and only two are in Condition 1. This may imply that environmental costs are putting pressure on water companies' dividend-paying ability. The coming of a more environmentally aggressive team to Washington, D.C., seems to imply no decrease in such pressure.

On the positive side, there are companies of all kinds—phone, gas, water, and electric—in the buyable categories, namely Conditions 1, 5, and 6 taken together. This is yet another reason there is no need for investors to reach for the highest-yielding stocks when choosing new utility stock positions.

Chart Sources

Long-Term Values. Computer-generated charts giving 12 years' history at a glance. Six consecutive issues update the entire universe of covered stocks. William O'Neil & Company, Inc., P.O. Box 66919, Los Angeles, CA 90066-0919.

SRC Blue Book. Logarithmic 12-year charts illustrating dividend and EPS trends, so following their growth rates need not require a calculator or computer. Securities Research Company, 101 Prescott Street, Wellesley, MA 02181.

Reference Materials

Moody's Dividend Record. Available at most public libraries. Annual issues helpful in projecting when a dividend increase should be anticipated. Includes frequent interim supplements in loose-leaf form. Moody's Investors Service, 99 Church Street, New York, NY 10007.

The Value Line Investment Survey. An excellent data source. Tends to be a bit optimistic on future dividend growth rates, so any cautious statements should be taken very seriously. Covers a large number of utilities, but not many of the smaller ones. Value Line, 711 Third Ave., New York, NY 10017-4064.

Mutual Fund Profiles. Highly authoritative reference published quarterly by a joint venture of Lipper Analytical Services, Inc., and Standard & Poor's Corp. Helpful in assessing the character, investment policy, and comparative actual returns of funds. Standard & Poor's Corp., 25 Broadway, New York, NY 10004.

Books

SBBI, 1926-1991. Chicago, IL: Ibbotson Associates, 1992. An annual update volume of the classic historical record of actual investment returns of various asset classes since 1926.

Fisher, Kenneth. *The Wall Street Waltz.* Chicago, IL: Contemporary Books, Inc., 1987. Long-term perspectives on economic cycles and interest rates through generous use of valuable charts.

Lorie, James H. and Hamilton, Mary T. *The Stock Market: Theories and Evidence.* Homewood, IL: Richard D. Irwin, Inc., 1973. Useful as a source for understanding the dividend discount model and general investment principles supporting the position that dividends are the primary determinant of equities' values.

Mamis, Justin. *The Nature of Risk.* New York, Addison-Wesley Publishing Company, Inc., 1991. A guide to measuring and thinking about uncertainty; highly enlightening for the nonprofessional and the practitioner alike.

Schwartz, James D. *Enough.* Englewood, CO: Labrador Press, 1992. A unique exploration of how much risk we need to take, what drives our desires for wealth, and how to forego unnecessary risk.

Slatter, John. *Safe Investing: How to Make Money Without Losing Your Shirt.* New York: Prentice-Hall, 1991. Provides yield and P/E performance parameters for conservative total-return investing; excellent summary of fundamentals important to utility investors as defined by a veteran brokerage analyst of utility stocks.

O'Glove, Thornton L. *Quality of Earnings*. New York, Macmillan, Inc., 1987. Provides revealing insights into accounting practices (not specific to utilities) that can embellish earnings. Another reason to rely on dividends as the primary signal.

APPENDIX III

	Attributes	Advantages	Risks
Electric	Highly Capital Intensive Process of consolidation via merger under way	Ubiquitous basic service Demand growth tied to long-term economic and population expansion Uneconomic to allow local competition	Some fuels pose environmental costs Specific nuclear risk Many company subject to single-state regulation unresolved electromagnetic radiation-cancer link
Gas	Clean; plentiful domestic supply Smaller minimum economic investment to add capacity	Relatively low coat Start of use as vehicle fuel	Demand more volatile than for electricity (due to economic cycles and weather) Danger of Explosion
Telephone	Capital intensive and increasingly "high-tech"	Age of the "information society" implies growth exceeding overall economy No dirty or dangerous aspects to supplying or delivering service	High-Tech nature means R&D and capital needed and change could drive obsolesecne Basic service highly politicized by advocates of poor and elderly
Water	Life sustaining Susceptible to contamination, with fear-inducing results	Essential Supply concerns imply price increases	Contamination Possible sabotage Environmental compliance rules change, raising costs For some, concept of profit on a necessity drives political activism and populist attitudes

APPENDIX IV

History of Returns on the S&P Industrial Utility Indexes

	S & P 45 Utilities				S & P 385 Industrials			
Year	Pct. Incr. Divds.	Cash Yield	Pct. Total Retn	Year-end Total Wealth Index	Pct. Incr. Divds.	Cash Yield	Pct. Total Retn	Year-end Total Wealth Index
1959				1.000				1.000
1960	5.1	4.16	19.8	1.198	5.3	3.10	-1.6	0.984
1961	5.4	3.79	29.0	1.546	4.0	3.38	26.5	1.245
1962	4.6	3.16	-2.6	1.506	5.8	2.91	-9.9	1.122
1963	5.4	3.54	12.3	1.691	8.2	3.61	23.7	1.387
1964	7.4	3.49	15.7	1.956	9.2	3.28	16.4	1.614
1965	7.3	3.34	4.7	2.047	9.6	3.18	13.1	1.825
1966	8.0	3.56	-4.6	1.953	4.6	3.03	-10.4	1.635
1967	6.3	4.12	-0.6	1.942	1.0	3.53	26.8	2.074
1968	4.5	4.52	10.0	2.136	5.6	3.03	10.5	2.293
1969	3.0	4.42	-15.1	1.813	2.8	2.89	-7.3	2.126
1970	2.9	5.65	15.7	2.098	-0.9	3.19	2.6	2.181
1971	2.5	5.27	2.2	2.144	-1.9	3.15	14.8	2.505
1972	1.8	5.53	7.6	2.306	1.3	2.86	19.9	3.003
1973	2.7	5.57	-17.6	1.901	8.1	2.64	-14.6	2.563
1974	1.8	7.38	-21.1	1.499	6.9	3.41	-26.5	1.884
1975	3.8	10.70	43.2	2.147	1.6	4.94	36.9	2.579
1976	4.7	8.46	30.5	2.802	12.4	4.21	22.6	3.163
1977	7.7	7.47	8.4	3.036	16.7	4.15	-8.2	2.902
1978	6.9	7.91	-3.5	2.929	7.9	5.11	7.5	3.120
1979	7.6	9.61	13.3	3.318	11.8	5.58	18.5	3.696
1980	6.4	9.87	14.3	3.791	9.5	5.41	33.1	4.919
1981	7.7	10.18	11.2	4.216	6.9	4.53	-6.7	4.588
1982	7.1	10.80	24.9	5.265	2.3	5.22	20.2	5.514
1983	5.8	10.01	19.5	6.290	2.9	4.68	22.8	6.772
1984	6.9	9.78	24.5	7.830	0.8	3.99	4.1	7.050
1985	4.0	8.87	31.6	10.307	4.2	4.15	30.0	9.165
1986	4.5	7.55	28.1	13.201	5.2	3.47	18.5	10.862
1987	5.0	6.57	-2.5	12.869	6.6	3.22	9.1	11.855
1988	3.3	7.46	17.7	15.153	12.3	3.41	15.8	13.728
1989	3.5	7.01	45.8	22.096	15.0	3.49	29.1	17.719
1990	5.1	5.30	-2.8	21.472	10.4	3.07	-0.9	17.555
1991	2.7	5.93	14.0	24.479	1.8	3.25	30.4	22.898
Best Year	8.0	10.80	45.8		16.7	5.58	36.9	
Worst Year	1.8	3.16	-21.1		-1.9	2.64	-26.5	
Mean	5.0	6.59	11.7		6.2	3.72	11.5	
Std. Dev.	1.9	2.43	15.9		4.5	0.82	15.7	
# Losses (of 32 years)			9				9	
Times down twice in row			2				1	

INDEX

N

natural gas distribution companies 65
natural gas transmission companies 64
natural gas utilities early-1993
  dividend signals 234
natural gas utilities' key characteristics and risks 64-66,84
Nevada Power 51,90,216
New England Electric System 77
New Jersey Resources 106
news media, influence of 60,154-155,
  186,191-192
Niagara Mohawk Power 90,101-102
Nine Mile Point nuclear project 101
NISPCO 90,100
non-nuclear electric companies,
  list of 189-190
nuclear power 43,50,61-62,84,153,
  185-190
Nuclear Regulatory Commission 187
NUI Corp. 106
NYNEX Corp. 67,181

O

obsolete nuclear plants: costs 188
Ohio Edison 90,216
omissions of dividends 61,65,70,82-
  84,87,90,96,99
omissions of dividends: surprising
  buy signal 119,130-132,146-
  147,166
one-decision investments 115
O'Neil, William & Co. 135,236
ONEOK 148
open access in telephone industry 67
open access to pipeline systems 64
opportunity cost 9,47,53
orphan stocks 174
overseas utilities, investing in 212

P

Pacific Enterprises 72,216
Pacific Gas & Electric 58,75-76,181
Panhandle Eastern 58
panic selling at bottoms 215
partnerships 178-180
payout ratios, high, as warning 67,
  86,105,117,124-125
Peoples Corp. 65
Philadelphia Electric 58,74,75-78,87
Philadelphia Suburban 68
Pinnacle West Capital 90,102-103,
  144,156-157
political impacts 41,50,57,60,112,
  163,164,187,223
preferred stocks 69-72,109
presidential election cycle 57,164
Price-Anderson Act 62,187
probabilities, long-term 23
projection, error of 111,160
prospectus of dividend reinvestment
  plan, value of 203-204
Providence Energy 65,170
PSI Resources 90,98-99
psychology on Wall St. 3,7,15,30,40,
  42,119,123,187,192
public relations 121,193,204
Public Service Enterprise Group 77
Public Service of Colorado 188
Public Service of New Hampshire 61,
  91-92,104,132
Public Service of New Mexico 90,
  105,187

R

rationalization 127,157,164,166
realistic expectations in
  investing 38,163
reasons for investing 1,2,7,237

About the Publisher

PROBUS PUBLISHING COMPANY

Probus Publishing Company fills the informational needs of today's business professional by publishing authoritative, quality books on timely and relevant topics, including:

- Investing
- Futures/Options Trading
- Banking
- Finance
- Marketing and Sales
- Manufacturing and Project Management
- Personal Finance, Real Estate, Insurance and Estate Planning
- Entrepreneurship
- Management

Probus books are available at quantity discounts when purchased for business, educational or sales promotional use. For more information, please call the Director, Corporate/Institutional Sales at 1-800-998-4644, or write:

Director, Corporate/Institutional Sales
Probus Publishing Company
1925 N. Clybourn Avenue
Chicago, Illinois 60614
FAX (312) 868-6250